MW01252305

MODERN WORLD NATIONS

Syria

Douglas A. Phillips

Series Editor
Charles F. Gritzner
South Dakota State University

An imprint of Infobase Publishing

Frontispiece: Flag of Syria
Cover: Shoppers at a bazaar in Damascus City, Syria

Syria
Copyright © 2010 by Infobase Publishing

Chelsea House
An imprint of Infobase Publishing
132 West 31st Street
New York NY 10001

Library of Congress Cataloging-in-Publication Data

Phillips, Douglas A.
  Syria / Douglas A. Phillips.
    p. cm. — (Modern world nations)
  Includes bibliographical references and index.
  ISBN 978-1-60413-617-3 (hardcover)
  1. Syria—Juvenile literature. I. Title.
  DS93.P48 2010
  956.91—dc22
                                2009043749

Chelsea House books are available at special discounts when purchased in bulk quantities for businesses, associations, institutions, or sales promotions. Please call our Special Sales Department in New York at (212) 967-8800 or (800) 322-8755.

You can find Chelsea House on the World Wide Web at
http://www.chelseahouse.com

Text design by Takeshi Takahashi
Cover design by Alicia Post
Composition by EJB Publishing Services
Cover printed by Bang Printing, Brainerd MN
Book printed and bound by Bang Printing, Brainerd MN
Date printed: April 2010
Printed in the United States of America

10 9 8 7 6 5 4 3 2 1

Table of Contents

Syria

CHAPTER

1

Introducing Syria

Syria is a country with many personalities. This makes it extremely confusing to many foreigners. Is it an ancient culture in modern times, a key player in today's Middle East, or a supporter of extremist Islamic terrorism and violence? Is it all three things and perhaps more? Perceptions of Syria vary widely, depending upon the source of information. For many Americans and others in the West, Syria represents an extremist Islamic society. For many in the Middle East, such as the Palestinians and Iranians, the country is a valued friend and ally. For travelers, Syria is a country blessed with an amazing history that can be matched by few other countries. This book delves into the mysteries of Syria and the Syrian people. It is hoped that the information in the following chapters will help raise the curtain of ignorance behind which the country has existed for so long in the Western mind.

Syria is a country located at the crossroads of Europe, Asia, and Africa. This location is very strategic. The powers that control these

Middle Eastern lands can control the vital gateway for movement between the continents. Historically, this location has been a very dangerous intersection. Many of the world's greatest civilizations and most powerful conquerors passed through today's Syria in their quest to control this strategic region. Even today, this continental crossroads is positioned in a very dangerous neighborhood.

Blessed or cursed by this location, Syria has thousands of years of history and an amazing culture. Its capital city, Damascus, is the world's oldest continuously inhabited urban center.

Syria is also a religious center for Christianity, Islam, and Judaism. Each of these faiths has deep roots in the country. For example, locations in Syria are mentioned many times in the Bible. Christianity's St. Paul was blinded and converted to Christianity on a road going to Damascus. Islam's founder, Muhammad, spent time in Syria. Today, the country is home to a predominately Shia Muslim population.

THE IMPORTANCE OF SYRIA'S LOCATION

The phrase "location, location, location" is often said in reference to real estate or the importance of location to some business or other economic activity. Location certainly played a vital role in Syria's past. It continues to do so today and certainly will in the future. For millennia, because of its location, Syria has experienced a constant flow of information, materials, and often trouble from the far reaches of the world.

The small country is sandwiched between Mesopotamia—the broad valley formed by the Tigris and Euphrates rivers—to the east, and the Mediterranean Sea to the west. Certainly few places in the world have played a more important role in molding world history than have Mesopotamia and those countries facing the Mediterranean Sea. Politically, Syria's neighbors are Turkey to the north, Iraq to the east, Jordan to the south, and Lebanon to the southwest. Through the ages and, in many respects, today, these four nations (along with Syria) have

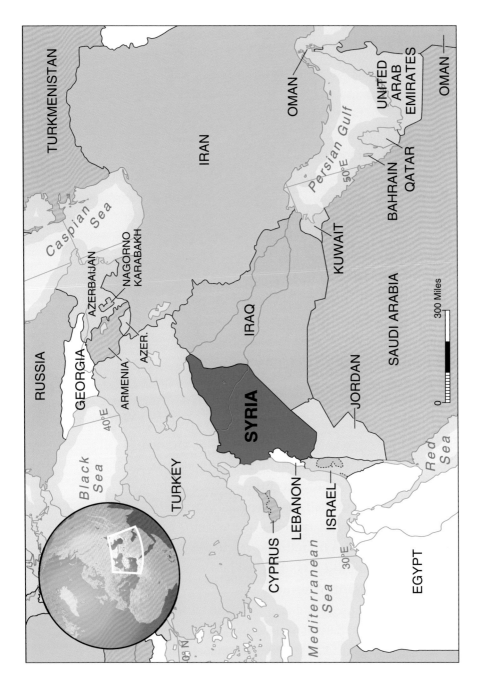

Syria is located in the Middle East, sharing borders with the Mediterranean Sea and Lebanon to the southwest, Turkey to the north, Iraq to the east, and Jordan to the south. Covering an area of 71,498 square miles (185,180 square kilometers), Syria is slightly larger than North Dakota.

played major roles on the stage of global affairs. Israel, Saudi Arabia, and Iran lie but a short distance away. Syria is in a challenging neighborhood in terms of both historical and present-day importance!

Of particular importance in terms of location is Syria's Mediterranean coastline of 120 miles (193 kilometers). This has given Syria a "window on the world," so to speak. Historically, various trade routes from the Indian Ocean, Persian Gulf, and Mesopotamia reached the Mediterranean by passing across present-day Syria. For several millennia, the famous Silk Road reached, among other coastal destinations, the Mediterranean through Syrian port cities. In addition to precious silk, a wealth of other materials and information reached the Middle East and ultimately Europe via this route. Today, Syria's location continues to serve a very strategic purpose. For example, two pipelines cross the country, transporting Middle Eastern oil to fuel Europe and places beyond. Throughout this book, as you learn about various topics, please keep in mind the importance of Syria's location.

Geographically, size does not necessarily equal strength. Small countries such as Syria, Israel, and the Netherlands, for example, have played a much greater role in world affairs compared to, say, places like Sudan, Africa's largest country. Syria is fairly small, relatively speaking. It occupies an area of 71,498 square miles (185,180 sq km), which includes those areas presently occupied by Israel. This makes it about the same size as North Dakota, or about one-third the size of Canada's Manitoba Province.

SYRIA'S PEOPLE

In 2009, Syria's population was estimated to be just over 20 million, giving it a population density of about 280 people per square mile (108 per sq km). In areas of varied terrain and climate, population density figures are rather meaningless, because there are not actually 280 people living in each square mile. Here, as elsewhere, people live under very crowded conditions in some favorable locations. The population is low in areas where it is difficult to make a living. Syria's population is comparable to that of New York State, although New York has a considerably higher population density. Syria's population is also rather young, averaging only 21.9 years of age. This is attributed to the country's high population growth rate, which ranks in the upper third of all countries.

Some Westerners believe negative ideas about Islam and Syrians. However, the Syrian people are among the kindest, most generous, and hospitable on the planet. Visitors invited to a Syrian home will encounter a very generous host and wonderful meals. Such an invitation should not be declined, as guests will have an evening that they will never forget.

Why, then, are so many Westerners wary of Syria and the Syrian people? Much of this can be attributed to a lack of knowledge about the people and their culture. Also, many actions of the Syrian government (a virtual dictatorship) reflect unfairly on the Syrian people. Ordinary Syrians have little say in the politics and foreign policy of the country. Syria's attempts to build nuclear devices, its support of Hizbollah extremists in Lebanon and Hamas terrorists in Palestine, and the allowed transport of anti-U.S. groups into Iraq are not voted on by the people. Citizens in Syria receive most of their media information from government-controlled sources. Therefore, it is difficult for them to find information contrary to government policy. Even if they can obtain this information, Syria's political structure includes few opportunities for citizens to exercise political participation.

The daily life of Syrians is a fascinating mix of Islam, family, friends, work, and other cultural elements. The government and the strong influence of the Ba'ath Party in politics will be explored, along with the stated rights of citizens. Actual rights may differ from stated rights since the society remains under the strong control of the Ba'ath Party.

In 2000, Syria experienced an *infitah*, or opening, when Western-trained Bashar al-Assad succeeded his father, Hafez, as president. The country saw the launch of its first independent newspapers in four decades and the display of lively discussions about reform and democracy in the state-owned media. Just a year later, privately owned papers were banned and the state-owned media went back to its old ways of censorship and restriction of information. Above, a Muslim imam preaches in a state-owned television studio in Syria.

As a country at the crossroads, it is important that we understand and monitor Syria and its very significant roles in the Middle East. This book will take you on a journey that travels back in time thousands of years, and then moves forward to peer into Syria's future. The expedition will look at key factors necessary for understanding the country today. Syria's saga is a compelling journey filled with bumps, opportunities, and turmoil. Let's get started!

2

Physical Landscapes

I n terms of its physical geography, Syria is very much like Southern California, minus that state's cool coastal current and frequent fog. Syria has a narrow coastal plain bordering upon the
Mediterranean Sea, and rather rugged terrain in the interior. Its climate is Mediterranean along the coast, giving way to parched desert
conditions in the interior. Fresh water resources are scarce, and precious where they do occur. As is true throughout Southern California,
most settlements are clustered around oasis sites, places where fresh
water is available. Water supplies in both locations are the source of
heated conflicts, both within the political unit and among several
neighbors.

Thus, Syria has one foot in the waters of the Mediterranean and
the other in arid desert landscapes. Other than that, few aspects of
Syria's physical geography stand out. In other words, the country

is neither helped nor hurt in any large measure by its natural conditions. (The one exception is perhaps Syria's lack of mineral resources other than petroleum and natural gas.) Although desert conditions dominate the country, the Euphrates River, its tributaries, and other streams provide adequate water for domestic consumption and irrigation.

LAND FEATURES

Syria's face on the Mediterranean is a rather narrow, low-lying coastal plain. Nowhere is it more than a few miles wide. Unlike Southern California, where the coastal plain is home to three huge cities, Syria's major urban centers are located inland. The rural population density on the coastal plain, however, is the highest in the country.

In the inland region, the hills and low mountains of the mountain range called Jabal an Nusayriyah run parallel to the coast. The southern range known as the Anti-Lebanon Mountains straddles the border with Lebanon. It descends to include the Golan Heights, a land area that is the center of a border dispute between Syria and Israel. Syria's highest point, Mount Hermon, is located in this range. It reaches an elevation of 9,232 feet (2,814 meters) and is frequently snow-covered at higher elevations during the winter months. The summit of Mount Hermon is under Syrian control, but portions of the range's southern slope have been under Israeli control since the Six-Day War in 1967. Syria's second-largest river, the Orontes, originates in the Anti-Lebanon Mountains in Lebanon. The waters flow northward from this source through Syria and into Turkey.

Important lowlands occupy east-central Syria, along the country's border with Iraq. Here, the Euphrates River and its tributaries have created a fertile alluvial valley with excellent soils. The rivers also provide ample water for irrigating crops. Al Jazira and Hawran are Syria's most important agricultural areas. It is this part of Syria that is considered to have been

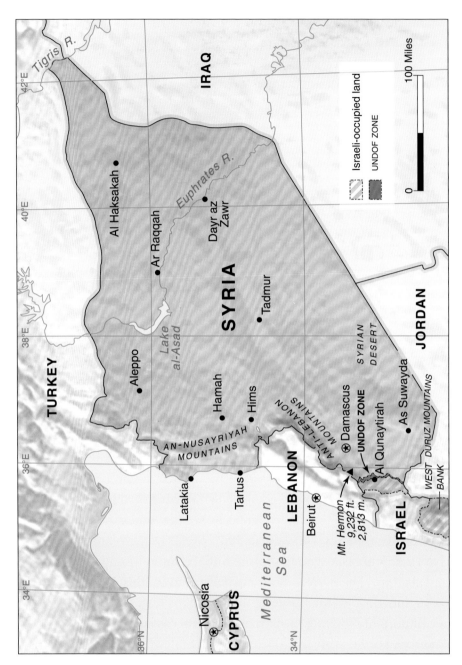

Syria's terrain comprises semiarid and desert plateau, narrow coastal plain, and mountains in the west. At 9,232 feet (2,814 meters), Mount Hermon, which is part of the Anti-Lebanon Mountains, is the country's highest point. There are also 42 Israeli-owned settlements and civilian land-use sites at the base of the range called the Golan Heights, which has been the focal point of conflict since 1967.

one of the ancient civilizations that were part of the so-called Cradle of Western Civilization.

WEATHER AND CLIMATE

Again, a comparison of conditions in Syria and those of Southern California can be useful in understanding the country's weather (the day-by-day conditions of the atmosphere) and climate (the long-range average of those weather conditions). Both areas lie about 30 to 35 degrees north latitude. The two regions also lie on the western side of mountain ranges. Conditions are very mild and pleasant. If asked what part of the United States has the most ideal climate, many Americans would respond "Southern California." Temperatures are moderate, with few harsh extremes. There is enough precipitation (although it varies by season), and storms are all but unknown. Both places share what is called a Mediterranean climate.

A major feature of the Mediterranean climate is that, unlike other climates, its dry season occurs during the summer months. In Southern California, an offshore cold-water current moderates summer temperatures. In contrast, coastal Syria experiences somewhat warmer summers that are also drier by comparison. Long periods may pass without a cloud in the sky. Weeks, or even months, may go by without precipitation. Along the coast, winter conditions are relatively mild and moist. Snow rarely falls at lower elevations, although it does happen on occasion. Damascus, for example, occasionally experiences sleet or snow. Snowfall and the build-up of snow are more frequent in highland areas. It is not uncommon for Mount Hebron to experience snowfall. In fact, both the Syrian and Israeli slopes of the mountain have skiing.

Inland, as is also true of Southern California, the pleasant Mediterranean climate gives way to arid desert conditions. Here, less than 10 inches (250 millimeters) of rain falls each year, and some places receive less than 5 inches (125 mm) of moisture. The land is parched and vegetation cover is scant. The range in temperature inland is much wider than along the coast. The average high temperature in Damascus in August is a sweltering 96°F (35.5°C), but during December it plunges to 33°F (0.6°C). The country's temperature extremes also have occurred at inland locations. Dayr Az Zawr, in east-central Syria, has recorded a sizzling 120°F (48.8°C); Hisyah, a community located at 4,372 feet (1,333 m) elevation, is Syria's coldest place, with a recording of 11°F (−11.7°C).

FLORA AND FAUNA

Humans have occupied present-day Syria for such a long period of time that little exists in terms of "natural" vegetation. Through cutting, burning, grazing, and farming, humans have completely altered the original vegetation patterns. Scrub, grasslands, and desert form the basic vegetation pattern as one moves from the more humid west to the drier interior. In the highlands, vegetation varies with elevation, and woodlands are able to grow in some upper elevations.

Wildlife, too, has been severely changed by humans. Very few "wild" species exist, other than the regional collection of birds, insects, and other small animals. The Mediterranean and several rivers are a source of fish and other aquatic life that are of local importance as a source of protein.

WATER FEATURES

Historically, Syria's face on the Mediterranean Sea has been very important to the country's physical environment, history, and economy. Physically, the sea is a source of moisture, and it moderates coastal temperatures. Historically, it has provided Syrians with a "window on the world."

Syrians have taken advantage of this window since ancient times. For several thousand years, the Phoenicians were among the world's most experienced and traveled seamen. It is not known how far they ventured. Some evidence exists that they traveled as far as the Americas and Asia. By 600 B.C., Phoenicians traveling under the directions of Egyptian king Necho sailed around Africa and successfully returned to the Mediterranean Basin.

The country's major river is the legendary Euphrates. The Euphrates and its tributaries serve the country with waters that have nourished the region and people for thousands of years. Even the Garden of Eden described in the Bible was supposedly nurtured by the Euphrates. The river starts in the highlands of eastern Turkey and flows 1,725 miles (2,776 km) through Turkey, Syria, and Iraq to where it empties into the Persian Gulf. Today, as in the past, the river serves as an economic life-blood for the country. It provides electrical energy and water for irrigation, creating a huge oasis that is the country's chief agricultural region.

Syria completed the Tabaqah Dam Project (also called the Thawra Dam Project) on the Euphrates in 1973. This created a large reservoir, Al-Assad Lake. Several other smaller dams also have been built on tributaries of the Euphrates. The precious water is used mostly for irrigation. Without this, crop agriculture would be all but nonexistent in most of the country. Upstream, Turkey has built more than 20 dams to control the flow of the Euphrates River. This potential control of the river's flow is a source of very hot political debate between the Turks and the downstream countries of Syria and Iraq.

The Orontes River, located in western Syria, has many rapids. It flows through narrow canyons throughout much of its course. As a result, it is of little use for navigation or irrigation. The Lake of Homs was created by the Al-Rastana Dam, the latest of many dams built at this location on the Orontes. The river's narrow valley has long served as an important north-south transportation corridor.

Since biblical times, the Euphrates River has been one of the most important rivers of Southwest Asia. Some historians place the Garden of Eden at the headwaters of the Euphrates and the Tigris (the other important river in Mesopotamia). Both Islamic and Christian prophecies claim that the Euphrates will dry up, causing major strife and war.

Scattered here and there throughout Syria's arid lands are oasis sites, places where good water is available at the land's surface. It can be in the form of a stream, spring water, ground water, or water diverted by canal from a distant source. The historic cities of Damascus and Palmyra are two of many Syrian cities that owe their existence to an oasis site.

THE FERTILE CRESCENT

The Fertile Crescent is an area that extends along the coast of the Mediterranean, reaches into a small portion of south-central Turkey, and curves southeastward into the Euphrates River Valley in northern and eastern Syria. From there it continues into Iraq. There, along with the Tigris River, it forms the fertile lands of Mesopotamia (a name that means "land between the rivers").

The region's nickname "Fertile Crescent" comes from its crescent shape. This is particularly meaningful because the crescent is a symbol of the Islamic faith. Countless important cultural developments occurred here. A few examples of these developments include some of the world's earliest documented agriculture and the world's first cities. These topics and more will be discussed at length in later chapters.

CHAPTER

3

Syria's Ancient Past

Ancient Syria occupied a much larger geographic area than the modern nation of Syria occupies today. The Greeks were the first to use the name *Syria* to refer to the key region on the eastern Mediterranean, where the three continents of Africa, Asia, and Europe join. Historians often refer to this Syria as *Greater Syria*, a term that includes not only the modern state of Syria but also Jordan, Israel, and Lebanon. Greater Syria was truly a crossroads, with the sea and three continents serving to link the region with most of the known world in ancient times. This prime location had both amazing advantages and discouraging disadvantages, many of which will be explored in this chapter.

EARLY SYRIAN CIVILIZATIONS

Bone fragments show that early humans were chasing after giant camels in the area of Syria around 100,000 years ago. Remains of these huge animals were found by Swiss researchers in El Kown, north of Damascus, in 2005. El Kown, in central Syria, is one of the oldest human settlements ever excavated. The researchers determined that the camels were a new species of giant dromedary, which are camels with one hump. The remains suggest that the camels were closer in size to giraffes and twice the size of normal camels. Human remains and tools made from animal foot bones have been found at the same site. It is believed that these humans had hunted the camels.

Early settlements in Syria were located along the mighty Euphrates River and existed 11,000 years ago during the Neolithic Period. Evidence of these early settlements includes the world's oldest wall painting, which was found at a Neolithic settlement on the Euphrates at Djade-al-Mughara. The painting was found in 2007 by French archeologists. Today, it is housed in a museum located in the nearby city of Aleppo. The painting has red, black, and white colors and provides firm evidence of human settlement and culture existing around 9000 B.C. These early people were hunters and gatherers who used flint (a very hard piece of quartz that produces a spark when struck by steel) and prehistoric weapons. According to archeologists, several of these Neolithic settlements existed, and they communicated and lived peacefully with each other.

Six thousand years ago, the start of a major city was formed in northeast Syria in the area of the modern city of Tell Brak. The Greeks used the legendary term *Mesopotamia* to refer to the area between the Tigris and Euphrates rivers. This is where the ancient settlement of Nagar was located. It became a major city before its demise around 1000 B.C. Referred to as the Brak/Nagar or Tell Brak site, the settlement featured donkey-pulled carts and traded with the city of Ebla. A colossal temple dating to 3500 to 3300 B.C. has been found at the archeological site at Tell Brak. The ruin is called the Eye Temple because of the thousands of peering stone eye idols found at the site. Today, the Eye Temple has been completely excavated, but the mystery of the meaning of the eyes continues to be unsolved.

The Kingdom of Ebla

In 1975, an Italian archeological team led by Professor Paolo Matthiae discovered the seeds of a great and extensive Syrian civilization at Tell Mardikh (Ebla). This site is 40 miles (64 km) south of the modern Syrian city of Aleppo and is named Ebla. The name *Ebla* means "white stones," a name that refers to the limestone rock on which the city was located.

The city was a major commercial center that traded with Mesopotamia and places as far away as Egypt. Its major trading competition was the Sumerian city of Mari; its main products were timber and textiles. The Ebla kingdom dominated northern Syria and twice conquered Mari. The kingdom also stretched at one point to include northern Syria, Iran, Anatolia, and lower Mesopotamia.

Ebla was a polytheistic society, which means that the people believed in many gods. The Eblaites elected their king for a fixed period of seven years. This tradition ended with Ibbi Sipish, the fifth king of Ebla, who made the throne inherited. Many believe that the absolute authority of the king, which was started by Ibbi Sipish, was responsible for the kingdom's downfall after his death. At that time, around 2300 B.C., Ebla fell to the Sumerian kingdom of Akkad. Nevertheless, Ebla rose again a few centuries later, around 1850 B.C.

When Matthiae and his Italian team discovered the site, the language of Ebla, called Eblaite, was unknown. Thousands of cuneiform tablets were found in the city's ruins, providing an immense source for unraveling the mysteries of the newly discovered language. Eblaite was a form of Sumerian with many new characters. It is now regarded as being the oldest written Semitic language.

Being at the continental crossroads frequently put Greater Syria at risk. The Amorites dominated the region around 2000

Ebla was a major commercial center that traded with peoples in Mesopotamia and as far away as Egypt, Iran, and Sumer. At the height of its power, Ebla controlled northern Syria, Lebanon, and parts of northern Mesopotamia (modern-day Iraq). In 1975, excavators found thousands of intact cuneiform tablets dating from 2250 B.C., written in a previously unknown Semitic language called Eblaite.

B.C. They were a nomadic people and are believed to have originated in Arabia. The Amorites fell when Egypt invaded Greater Syria and brought much of the region under its power. The Hittites also ruled Syria at various times during the centuries, from 1600 to 1200 B.C. Both the Egyptians and Hittites were seeking to extend their empires, and thus had a strong influence over the affairs of Greater Syria for nearly four centuries.

One reason for the ease with which these powers took Greater Syria is that city-states were still widespread in the region. These smaller powers could not match the military might of kingdoms that possessed greater land area and population.

Damascus: Syria's Ancient City

Damascus is Syria's capital city. Its roots are very deep and date back to nearly 15,000 B.C. The city was first settled on an oasis around 2500 B.C. and has been inhabited since that time. Archeological findings at Tell Ramad, an area on the outskirts of Damascus, indicate that the location was a city-state nearly 13,000 years ago. However, Damascus did not become important until nomadic Aramaeans arrived from Mesopotamia. Since that time, the city has served as a key center for religion, politics, education, and commerce. It claims to be the world's oldest continuously inhabited city.

Hammurabi and Babylonia

Also influencing Syrian kingdoms was the Babylonian kingdom, located between the Tigris and Euphrates rivers in what is modern-day Iraq. Hammurabi, king of Babylon in the eighteenth century B.C., extended his kingdom's reach into Syria during his reign. During the second millennium B.C., Greater Syria served as a marchland, which means a land between two or more often-competing powers. Greater Syria was a marchland for powers including the Canaanites, Phoenicians, Egyptians, Hittites, Babylonians, and Assyrians.

The Assyrians conquered Damascus in 732 B.C. Their rule was short. Babylonia, led by Nebuchadnezzar II, retook Syria in 612 B.C. Thus, governance and control of Greater Syria was like a revolving door for centuries, as Syria's location served to make the region a doormat for more powerful states.

Persians and Greek Macedonians

Other world powers continued to tread over Syria, including the Persians, who arrived in the sixth century B.C. The Persians were more tolerant of local rule than past powers, but their reign ended in 333 to 332 B.C. when Alexander the Great conquered them. Alexander was a Greek who was king of Macedon, then a part of the Greek empire. He was able to seize not only Greater Syria but also the ancient Greek city-states, Egypt, and Mesopotamia. He even reached distant India.

Alexander's conquests brought not only new rulers, but also the first major infusion of Western ideas and institutions to Greater Syria. Alexander encouraged his soldiers to marry foreign women. He followed this policy himself by marrying two foreign princesses. Alexander conquered most of the known world during his reign. He died at the young age of 33 under circumstances that are still questioned today. At the time of his death, Greater Syria was part of Alexander's empire.

The Greek influence of Alexander the Great has impacted Syria in a number of ways. First, after conquering Greater Syria, many Greeks moved into the area. New cities were spawned, and Western thinking in philosophy, science, and law were introduced. The Greek language was also spread into the region, along with new technology that provided for better roads and more reliable water sources.

By the end of the fourth century B.C., Greater Syria had been taken over by one of Alexander's generals. The general, Seleucus I, founded his new capital at Antioch. Antioch remained the Seleucid capital and later became the kingdom of Syria. The Seleucids further spread Greek ideas into the kingdom, but mostly to just the upper classes. The kingdom of Syria remained under Seleucid rule until the Romans, under Pompey, conquered the region in 64 B.C. and made Syria a Roman province.

The Romans

The Romans ruled more harshly than previous masters had ruled. The European power was determined to root out other competing powers in the region. These enemies included the Palmyrenes in central Syria and the Parthians to the east. The

Romans forced Syrians into the military and made them slaves in their efforts to defeat these enemies and to extend the Roman Empire. The Romans eventually defeated the Palmyrenes, but they never completely defeated the Parthians, who were located in modern-day Iran.

The Romans brought their religion to Syria. Roman religion was a collection of beliefs and practices that had more in common with cults. Their religions were mainly polytheistic, with many gods. The Romans also were not tolerant of religions that were monotheistic (having a belief in only one god). This policy soon came into conflict with religions that were spawned in the Middle East and found accepting audiences in Syria.

Judaism and the new faith spread by Jesus Christ and his disciples were more common in Syria after the turn of the millennium. Christianity was spreading quickly, and much of this was due to a Jew named Saul, who later became St. Paul. St. Paul converted from Judaism to Christianity while he was on the road to Damascus in A.D. 33. He was on a mission to hunt down and persecute Christians in Damascus when, according to the Bible, he was overcome with a blinding light. God then spoke to him and said, "Saul, why do you persecute me?" Paul describes his conversion to Christianity in the New Testament of the Bible. After being blinded by the searing, bright light and hearing God's voice, he was baptized in Damascus. He later stayed with Christians there for three years and preached.

St. Paul's conversion led him to spread Christianity to many areas of the eastern Mediterranean. Eventually, he ran into the wrath of the Romans when Emperor Nero was persecuting Christians. Thus, St. Paul's death came quickly at the hands of Nero's tyranny. St. Paul was caught and beheaded around A.D. 67. The impact of his writings and his conversion to Christianity in Syria has affected billions of Christians around the world.

On the right bank of the Orontes River is the ancient city of Apamea. It is notable for its long Roman street lined with classical columns. From 64 B.C. to A.D. 636, Syria was a Roman province, and much of what remains today in Apamea was built by the Romans. The ruins also include shops, a bath house, some villas, and a small amphitheater. As a major trade route with the Far East, many distinguished visitors came to this important city, including Cleopatra.

Roman rule under Emperor Constantine embraced Christianity in A.D. 313. This spurred numerous church construction projects in Syria. Also during Roman rule, the population of Syria exploded, as the region was very prosperous. Three Syrians even became Roman emperors, since the status of Syria was very high in the Roman Empire. The three emperors were Elagabalus (emperor from A.D. 218–222), Marcus

Aurelius Severus Alexander (A.D. 222–235), and Marcus Julius Philippus (A.D. 244–249).

The Roman Empire split into two pieces in A.D. 395. The Western Roman Empire was governed by Rome. The Eastern Roman Empire, also called the Byzantine Empire, had its capital in Constantinople, a city named after Emperor Constantine. This city is today Istanbul, Turkey. Syria remained a part of the Byzantine Empire until A.D. 636, when it was conquered by Arabs who were expanding their Islamic Empire. Thus, Syria was again at the continental crossroads, with religion being a source of conflict between Christianity and the new religion called Islam.

ANCIENT SYRIA AT THE CROSSROADS—AGAIN?

The amazing story of ancient Syria shows the dilemma posed by being at the continental intersection and next to the Mediterranean Sea. On the one hand, the region was a center for trade and ideas that moved between regions and powers. On the other hand, Syria was always in the center of conflicts between larger powers and influences that swept over the known world during ancient times. Will these patterns continue in the era after the Romans and Byzantine Empire, or will Syria find stability and use its location for new advantages? The answer to this question and others will be explored in Chapter 4.

CHAPTER

4

Syria Enters Modern Times

The contradictory legacies of Syria's location have presented Syrians with many challenges and opportunities. Ancient times found Greater Syria frequently occupied by foreign powers. Yet there were also opportunities to learn new ideas, participate actively in trade, and establish strong institutions. Syria, however, frequently suffered at the hands of outside powers that had superior militaries and technology. Syria's pattern of being conquered and influenced would continue for many centuries.

THE UMAYYAD CALIPHATE

The Byzantine Empire lost control of Syria in A.D. 636. By this time the Byzantines had ruled Syria for 240 years. Byzantine rule was followed by outside Islamic rulers who conquered the area in A.D. 636 in the Battle of Yarmuk. By A.D. 661, Damascus had been selected to be the residence of the Umayyad caliph named Muawiyah. This meant that Syria became the central region of the Umayyad Empire. The Umayyad Caliphate was the second of the Islamic caliphates established after the death of the Prophet Muhammad, who had begun the religion of Islam. Muhammad died in A.D. 632, but his followers quickly spread the faith from Arabia across the Mediterranean Sea and eastward into Syria and the Middle East. The role of Islam in Syria today is discussed further in the next chapter.

A caliphate was an Islamic form of government that respected religious and political unity in the Muslim-controlled world. A caliph is the person who controls the territory in a caliphate. In most Western societies, there is a division between government and religion; however, the caliphates used Muhammad's teachings from the holy Koran to govern. This meant that they would use words of the Koran as law. This is usually referred to as sharia law, which many Westerners believe is too strict and sometimes violates human rights. The four major roles of the caliph were to serve as the caliphate's spiritual, religious, political, and military leader. Thus, even today, religion and government in most Islamic countries are closely tied together.

The caliphate centered in Syria existed from A.D. 661 until 750. At its peak, the empire stretched from Spain to India. With Damascus as the home of Caliph Muawiyah I, Syria prospered. He was considered to be a political and military genius. Muawiyah I expanded the Islamic Empire by expelling the Byzantines and by conquering Muslim neighbors. He created a professional army and navy that were both well trained and paid regularly. Caliph Muawiyah I also was very tolerant of Christians and allowed them to serve in the military. He also appointed many Christians to high political offices. This was important since many Christians lived in Syria at that time. Syrians today still hold tremendous respect for Muawiyah because he demonstrated many desirable qualities, including

The Umayyad family originally came from the holy city of Mecca and made Damascus their home. The Umayyads established the largest Arab-Muslim state and built some of the most famous buildings in the world, including the Dome of the Rock in Jerusalem and the Umayyad Mosque (*pictured, center*), also known as the Grand Mosque, in Damascus.

tolerance, self-discipline, and generosity. He also is credited with having made Damascus a more beautiful city.

Some Muslims view Muawiyah as a companion of Muhammad and think highly of him. Other Muslims dislike Muawiyah, since they believe that his conversion to Islam was questionable. They contend that Muawiyah used Islam as a means of obtaining political power and material gains. Thus, even today, he is a figure who divides opinions in Islamic countries. His death in A.D. 680 from a stroke allowed his designated heir, his son Yazid, to become caliph. However, both Yazid and Muawiyah's grandson, Muawiyah II, died early. As a result, the caliphate quickly passed on to another descendent, Marwan I, who also died young. This left the caliphate to Abd al-Malik, the son of Marwan I.

Abd al-Malik became the fifth caliph and ruled for two decades, until A.D. 705. He is viewed as one of the greatest Muslim caliphs. He was responsible for the construction of the Dome of the Rock in Jerusalem, which was completed in A.D. 691. This shrine is the oldest Islamic building in the world and hovers over the Jewish religious site called the Wailing Wall in the old city of Jerusalem. Abd al-Malik also reasserted control over the caliphate with numerous military victories and by quashing rebellions that occurred. He increased the size of the caliphate in North Africa and made Arabic the official language of government across the empire.

Abd al-Malik's son, Al Walid I, was also an effective ruler who stretched the boundaries of the caliphate to their greatest levels. This included reaching across the Mediterranean Sea into Spain and Portugal. He is responsible for constructing the mosque at Damascus and initiating a renaissance in Islamic architecture. He further linked Islam and the Arabic language and made Arabic the *only* official language in the caliphate. He was also the first to coin an Islamic currency. This monetary system was used across the Muslim world.

After Al Walid I, the next significant caliph was Hisham ibn Abd al-Malik, who ruled from A.D. 723 until his death in A.D. 743. He encouraged the arts and spread education by building schools. Many literary works were translated into Arabic. Al-Malik governed with simplicity and honesty, but he also worked to implement a stricter version of sharia law. During al-Malik's reign, rebellions against the caliphate became more frequent in the more remote areas of the empire. The end of the Umyyad caliphate came a few years later with the arrival of the Abbasids.

THE ABBASID CALIPHATE

The Abbasids were gaining power at the time of Hisham ibn Abd al-Malik's death. This group based their efforts on the belief that Abbas ibn 'Abd al-Muttalib, an uncle of Muhammad, was a more legitimate heir to the caliphate, rather than Muawiyah. Their candidate for caliph was a descendent of al-Muttalib named As-Saffah. As-Saffah was the first Abbasid caliph. His rule changed Syria because the Abbasid forces conquered the Umayyad caliphate that had ruled for so long.

In A.D. 750, the Abbasid caliphate moved the caliph's residence to Baghdad, which is today the capital of Iraq. This caliphate represented a golden era for Islam, with the empire stretching across Africa, the Middle East, and into Asia.

The Abbasids embraced the importance of education. Quickly, the empire became the intellectual center for medicine, philosophy, and sciences such as astronomy and mathematics. In fact, Abbasid Persian Al-Khwarizmi is considered by most to be the father of algebra. The Abbasids also translated many literary works into Arabic. These included works from Euclid, Plato, Aristotle, Hippocrates, and others. Without these translation efforts, many important literary works would have been lost. In addition, the root stories for *One Thousand and One Nights* (also called *Arabian Nights* in the West) started during this time period and provided the foundation for preserving many caliphate folk tales.

The Abbasids also excelled with technology. Among their creations were the windmill, crankshaft, watermill, and many other inventions. They also captured the power of moving water by the use of dams, as well as harnessing tidal, wind, and steam power for industrial production. At the crossroads of trade among Africa, Asia, and Europe, the Abbasids also modified and improved technology developed elsewhere. These technologies included paper, gunpowder, and irrigation, as well as improved agriculture and manufacturing processes.

SYRIA AND THE CRUSADES

Between 1097 and 1144, the first Crusaders arrived from Western Europe. They incorporated western areas of Syria into the Kingdom of Jerusalem, which was Christian. The Crusaders had seen many important Christian historical sites fall under the control of Muslims. Thus, the Crusades were designed to seize many of these sites, including the city of Jerusalem itself. However, Jerusalem is also the third-most important city to Muslims. Saladin, founder of the Ayyubid caliphate of Egypt, was successful in pushing the Crusaders out of Syria and then Jerusalem in 1187. Saladin became very popular in Syria and improved the economy. But his rule there fell into disarray after his death from malaria. Soon after his death, parts of Syria broke into smaller Ayyubid states.

MONGOLS INVADE AND INVADE . . .

The rule of the Abbasids ended in 1258 when the Mongols, led by Hulagu Khan (grandson of Genghis Khan, the famous Mongol leader), invaded and sacked the city of Baghdad. They also attacked the Ayyubid states in Syria that had existed in the area since 1174. Hulagu Khan's attacks also weakened the influence of Damascus and Aleppo, which were among the captured cities. The Mongols used their fighting forces and the populations of poor Christians to conquer Muslim Syria and the Ayyubid caliphate in 1260. Their rule and frequent invasions devastated the irrigation systems and cities and left the area in shambles.

Hulagu had intended to capture other regions, such as Egypt, but the Mongol Great Khan Mongke, Hulagu's older brother, died in 1259. This meant that Hulagu was required to return home to participate in the councils that would select a new Great Khan. Former Turkish slaves called Mamluks challenged the Mongol forces that were left behind. A second Mongol invasion occurred in 1271, but the Mamluks were successful in pushing the invading forces back beyond the Euphrates River. A third Mongol invasion had a similar result in 1281. The Mongols continued their pursuit of Syria with invasions in 1299 and 1303, when they were defeated in their last major invasion of the region. Mongol efforts to invade and control Syria had continued for nearly a half century. The invaders were never able to hold the territory for long time periods. The Mamluk sultans mainly ruled the region until the arrival of a new power, the Ottoman Turks.

THE OTTOMAN TURKS

During the early sixteenth century, the new dominant power in Syria's part of the world was the Ottoman Turks. By 1516, Syria had been incorporated into the Ottoman Empire, where it remained for nearly 400 years. The Turkish city of Constantinople (now called Istanbul) was the capital of the Ottoman Empire. The empire stretched into Europe, North Africa, the Middle East, and to Asia's doorstep by the Caspian Sea. The Ottoman Turks were Muslims, as their society had been converted in the eighth century by Umayyad conquerors.

The Ottoman Turks used pashas to rule over Syria. Pashas were military and administrative leaders who ruled with absolute authority. Syrians did not object forcefully to the Ottoman rule because these new rulers spoke Arabic and were Muslim. Damascus actually benefited, as the city became an important stop for travelers. Many travelers were Muslims going on their Hajj, or holy pilgrimage to Mecca, from other parts of the empire.

In other ways, however, the economy of Syria suffered under the Ottoman Empire. Aleppo surpassed Damascus in terms of economic importance and trade. This started a rivalry between the two cities that continues even today. With the trade activity that did take place, foreigners such as the

Jamal Pasha (*left, in carriage, riding through Damascus*), also known as Jamal the Butcher, was governor and commander of the Ottoman army in Syria during World War I. He ordered the execution of Lebanese and Syrian Shia Muslims and Christians on May 6, 1916, in Damascus and Beirut, Lebanon. That day is now commemorated as Martyrs Day, a national holiday in Syria and Lebanon.

French came to Syria and brought their missionaries, teachers, and other settlers into the region. Soon, these foreigners were demanding rights to their own religion and other protections. Sultan Sulayman I granted various rights to Christians and the French in 1535. The British gained similar rights in 1580. In the eighteenth century, Russia was granted similar religious rights for Orthodox Christians. Thus, Syria's Christian community was gaining a significant foothold that would continue in later centuries.

The influences of Western European countries in Syria increased in the nineteenth century. At the same time, the power of the Ottoman Turks was declining. The French built railroads in Syria and sent in troops during a revolt in the Syrian province of Lebanon in 1860. In 1861, Lebanon was taken away from Syria and fell increasingly under the influence of France. The building of the Suez Canal in 1869 also affected Syria as land trade routes in the region became less important and efficient.

The last Ottoman sultan with ultimate power was Sultan Abdul Hamid II. His reign was marked by cruelty and oppression. He increased taxes and persecuted his enemies. In addition, it was under his rule that an estimated 100,000 Armenians were massacred by his troops. After a failed assassination attempt in 1905, he was removed as sultan in 1909. His successor died in 1918 and was followed by the last Ottoman Turk sultan, Mehmed VI, who lost the once great Ottoman Empire in 1922.

SYRIA UNDER THE FRENCH

The increasing influence of the French in the nineteenth century in Syria came to an end for the European power in the twentieth century. World War I broke out in 1914, and many Arabs wanted to rid themselves of Ottoman rule. The last remnants of the Ottoman Empire sided with the Central Powers (Germany, Austria-Hungary, and Bulgaria) in the war. Arabs, however, believed that joining the Allies was their best path to independence. This meant that they became allies with the United Kingdom and France.

In 1916, however, the United Kingdom and France, plus Russia, had signed a secret pact called the Sykes-Picot Agreement. This treaty established so-called spheres of influence for France and Britain. The secret agreement provided for the French and the British to divide up Arab lands after the Ottoman Empire fell. Syria and Lebanon would fall under the influence of the French, while Jordan and Iraq would go to the British. Russia was also to receive control of areas around Constantinople and nearby provinces. France and Britain suspended the Russian parts of the agreement in 1917 because of the Russian Revolution.

Syrian nationalists (a nationalist is a political party or group that supports national independence) took control of their country, believing that Syria had a path open for independence since it was on the side of the Allies in World War I. Instead, the path suddenly took a turn in another direction. Prince Feisal, son of the Grand Sharif of Mecca (a term for governor and protector of the Islamic holy cities of Mecca and Medina) and a companion of British captain Thomas Lawrence (featured in the film *Lawrence of Arabia*), took control of Syria after the city of Damascus fell to Arab fighters in 1918. Feeling betrayed by the Sykes-Picot Agreement, Feisal led a rebellion and became the first king of Greater Syria in March 1920.

His reign was short. Only four months later, the French stepped in and defeated Feisal's army at Maysalun. The French then expelled Feisal, and this transition meant that the French now ruled Syria. The rule of the Ottoman Turks had indeed been shed, only to have another appear: the French. The British later installed Feisal as the king of Iraq in 1921.

Syrian nationalists promoted independence for the country, but the French ruled for more than two decades after Feisal's defeat. The League of Nations (an intergovernmental organization established by the peace treaties that ended World War I) put Syria under French control in 1922, which confirmed the international community's agreement with French rule in Syria and Lebanon. Still, Syrian resistance to the French continued, with the most noteworthy uprising taking place from 1925 to 1927.

In Europe, storm clouds were building during the 1930s with the growing menace of Nazi Germany. European powers such as the French and British needed fewer distractions from their distant lands. This meant that nationalist movements in places like Syria gained greater credibility and support. Thus, in 1938, the French and Syrians negotiated a treaty agreement that provided steps toward independence. Then, however, the French government refused to formally approve the agreement, as they took another look at the situation and determined that Syria would provide a strategic military position for the war. Many Syrians reacted strongly against this treaty, but most chose to support France and the Allies as World War II broke out in 1939.

Syria's fortunes changed greatly in 1940 when France fell to Nazi Germany. The Germans set up a puppet government in France, which is referred to as Vichy France. A puppet government is controlled by an outside authority and may impose hardships upon those it governs. Germany controlled Vichy France, and therefore held control of Syria. This situation rapidly changed later in 1940 when the British and Free French forces took Syria and Lebanon back from the Germans. (French fighters continued fighting against Axis forces after German occupation.) The Free French were then put in control of Syria. Now supported by the Free French and British, Syria declared independence in 1941. The French, however, periodically tried to reestablish their influence up until 1946 when their last soldiers left.

INDEPENDENCE!

Syria's bumpy path to independence was long and difficult. Independence was preceded by centuries of outside control. These included both ancient and modern groups, and some of the greatest powers in history. Among them were the Canaanites, Phoenicians, Aramaeans, Egyptians, Sumerians, Assyrians, Babylonians, Hittites, Persians, Greeks, Romans, Ottoman Turks, and the French. After centuries of being ruled by others, the time for a self-governing country of Syria had finally arrived. It was recognized as an independent republic in

1944 and became a charter, or original, member of the United Nations in 1945. The new country, since it had also formally joined the Allies in 1945, found itself on the winning side of World War II.

The early years of independence were very rocky, marked by upheaval and many government takeover attempts. Most of these attempts were led by the military, with some being successful. Internal politics also divided the country, as there were four constitutions and a startling 20 cabinets leading the government between 1946 and 1956.

NEW NATIONS CLASH

The United Nations created the state of Israel, and on May 14, 1948, the country declared its independence. This action was strongly rejected by the Arabs whose lands had been carved up and taken to create Israel. Israel's day of independence triggered an Arab attack that included forces from Egypt, Syria, Lebanon, and Jordan. The war ended in 1949, but without a peace agreement. Instead, the United Nations enforced an armed truce between the warring parties.

Tragically, more than 400,000 Palestinians had been displaced by the war and pushed out of Palestine. They remain without a home country to this day. Thus, the seeds of this modern-day problem were first planted by this war between Israel and surrounding Arab nations.

As the Palestinian issue festered in the 1950s, France, the United Kingdom, and the United States became strong supporters of Israel. The Soviet Union (today called Russia) supported Arab interests. In this way, the Middle East became involved in Cold War issues that divided the world in many places. In 1956, Israel launched a massive invasion of Egypt's Sinai Peninsula, with the support of the French and British.

Syria, meanwhile, had increasingly been turning away from Western powers because of the Palestinian issue and the new attack on Egypt. This meant that the Syrians were drawing closer to the Soviet Union. In 1957, the United States proclaimed the Eisenhower Doctrine, which sought to keep Soviets and Communists out of the Middle East. Syria denounced the U.S. policy. By the end of the 1950s, Syria had developed a much closer relationship with the Soviet Union and more hostile feelings toward the United States, United Kingdom, and France.

Conflicts between Israel and its neighbors were frequent during the second half of the twentieth century. Another major conflict, called the Six-Day War, broke out in 1967. Syria, Jordan, and Egypt, supported by other Arab nations, suffered a humiliating loss in a war that lasted only 132 hours, from June 5–10. At the end of the fighting, the Israeli forces were less than 31 miles (50 km) from Damascus and had captured the strategic Golan Heights in Syria, in addition to the Sinai Peninsula in Egypt, the Gaza Strip between Egypt and Israel, the West Bank in Palestine, and East Jerusalem, which had been controlled by Jordan since 1948. This devastating Arab defeat meant that more lands were lost to the Israelis. As a result of the war, the Suez Canal, a vital waterway linking the Mediterranean Sea and the Red Sea, was closed for eight years.

A NEW UNION OR NOT?

Egyptian and Syrian ties had long been strong in a bond of Arab unity that had existed for centuries. This idea was advanced even further by the invasion of the Sinai Peninsula and Israeli intrusion onto Arab lands. In 1958, elections were held in Egypt and Syria that proposed a union between the two countries. The resolution passed overwhelmingly, and a federation of the two countries called the United Arab Republic (UAR) was created. Gama Abdel Nasser of Egypt served as president of the new union. Land reforms were carried out, and steps were taken toward unification. But then, on September 28, 1961, Syrian army units seized control of Damascus and proclaimed a new independent Syria.

The Six-Day War was fought between the Israeli army and the armies of the neighboring states of Egypt, Jordan, and Syria. Israel conquered and captured several Arab territories, a devastating loss to the Arab nations that continues to affect the region's politics today. Above, Israeli troops raise their flag that has been planted on Syrian territory in June 1967.

The 1961 takeover was followed by others, which created a tumultuous decade of violence and internal power struggles in Syria. Finally, in 1970, Minister of Defense Hafez al-Assad led a bloodless takeover of the government that put al-Assad and the Ba'ath Party in control. This meant that the UAR idea had long expired. A new element had taken leadership in Syria, led by a moderate and conservative element consisting of the Ba'ath Party and al-Assad.

THE ERA OF HAFEZ AL-ASSAD

The Ba'ath Party takeover in 1970 began the 30-year rule of Hafez al-Assad. His leadership was to be marked by increasing dictatorial practices that were supported and carried out by the Ba'ath Party. It is true that he did bring stability to the country after decades of takeovers and chaos and turned a relatively small country into a major regional player; however, he also ruled with an iron fist and promoted himself to the point of hero worship that pervaded most aspects of Syrian society. He would bribe, threaten, or destroy rivals and would use intimidation to create fear in possible challengers.

In October 1973, al-Assad conspired with Egypt and other Arab countries to conduct a surprise attack upon Israel. This war is called the Yom Kippur War by Israelis and the Ramadan War by Arabs. Early Arab victories pushed the Israelis back from the Golan Heights and the Sinai lands that they had taken in the 1967 war. By the second week, however, the Israelis had pushed back and retaken the Golan Heights just before a United Nations cease-fire took effect. Although Syria did not regain the land it had lost in the 1967 war, the early victories did leave Syrians and other Arabs feeling better after the humiliating defeat in the Six-Day War.

In 1979, the United States, under President Jimmy Carter, helped negotiate a peace agreement between Egypt and Israel. The agreement was called the Camp David Accords. With this agreement, Egypt became the first Arab nation to start having normal diplomatic relations with Israel. The impact of the Camp David Accords was huge in the Middle East and led later to an agreement between Jordan and Israel. Syria, however, still does not have formal recognition or relationships with Israel even today.

President Hafez al-Assad developed a police state (a state in which the government rigidly controls the social, political, and economic life of its people), but he also made advances in the country. The Thawra Dam was constructed on the Euphrates River, and other infrastructure was built. Education was extended to more segments of the population, and living standards increased. He maintained close relations with the Soviet Union until that regime fell. He also frequently meddled in Lebanon's internal politics, seemingly unable to keep his hands off the former Syrian land, which had been independent since 1943. Starting in 1982, Syria had troops stationed in Lebanon. They continued to pull political and military strings into the twenty-first century. They also moved thousands of Syrians into Lebanon in a stealth attempt to colonize the country. Al-Assad died on June 10, 2000, after 30 years of ruling Syria. His death marked the end of an era. What, Syrians wondered, would come next?

NEW QUESTIONS AND A NEW ERA

Hafez al-Assad was followed by a temporary president who was in office for only a little more than a month. Uncontested elections brought al-Assad's son, Bashar al-Assad, into the presidency. The election spurred hope in Syria and in Western countries that his leadership would be more tolerant and liberal than his father's presidency. This hope was based on the fact that Bashar had not been greatly involved in politics before becoming president. In fact, he had been virtually absent from public life, and known for his modern Western outlook resulting from his British education in the 1980s.

Here, a boy holds posters of Syrian president Bashar al-Assad *(left)* and his father, former president Hafez al-Assad. For 30 years, Hafez was a feared and respected leader who ruled Syria with an iron fist. When he died in 2000, people hoped that his son Bashar's leadership would lead to political and economic reforms.

Bashar has made some reforms in Syria, but these were limited in the early years of his presidency. New efforts by the United States to reach out to Syria may hold promise, as Syria appears poised to become more engaged in the international community in positive ways. This is important because Syria was subjected to U.S. sanctions, or penalties, starting in 2004 because of Syria's stand on the U.S. invasion of Iraq earlier in that year. The installation of President Barack Obama in 2009 provided new doorways for discussion between Syria and the United States, as U.S. foreign policy worked to establish better relations. Thus, at the end of the first decade of the twenty-first century, there is the potential for improved relations between Syria and the United States.

A LONG HISTORY

Syria has a history that goes back millennia, marked by many foreign rulers and, finally, independence. Most recently, it suffered under political instability that lasted until the 30-year reign of Hafez al-Assad. With his more moderate son Bashar now ruling, the country seems poised for a more cooperative future with the West and with Israel. Both public and private discussions with the United States took place in 2009. This could lead to a more peaceful and stable Middle East and to Syria being more active in the international community. The world will remain hopeful, waiting to see what the results of these negotiations will be.

5

People
and Culture

An enchanting melody carries across the light evening air and echoes down the busy streets and alleys of Damascus. The voice that is singing is beckoning fellow Muslims and reminding them that it is time for prayer. This call to prayer, called the *adhan*, is offered five times each day, a call to Muslims to pray to Allah. The adhan is one of the many cultural elements found in Syria and is one that is repeated in Muslim nations around the world.

The culture of a country is a vitally important area of study for geographers. It allows for the examination of those human elements or flavors that make societies similar in some ways and different in others. The foundation of Syrian culture is thousands of years old, but it is not unchanging. New elements are added, and influences have come from the many invaders and traders that came through the country in generations past. This means that the Romans, Ottoman

Turks, Arabs, French, and many others have all left their finger-prints on the people and culture of Syria.

This cultural examination of the people of Syria will consider the language, customs, beliefs, foods, social practices, literature, music, education, sports, and arts in the country. The exploration will travel into the daily life and practices of Syrians and the joys, pleasures, and even potential pitfalls that visitors can experience when traveling there. For Westerners, this trip into the culture of Syria will present exciting information to better understand how Syrians live.

SYRIA'S PEOPLE

Who are Syria's people? Statistics provide one snapshot of a country's people. Aside from statistics, however, there is other information that provides a glimpse at important cultural dimensions of the population. This other information can include language, religion, gender issues, diet, and other factors. Pay close attention in order to learn that Syrians have many similarities to and differences from other people around the world.

Population

Estimates in mid-2009 indicated that the population of Syria was just over 20.1 million. In addition to this figure are the 40,000 people living in the Golan Heights, which was still occupied by Israel at the end of the first decade of the twenty-first century. This population figure is about 2 million more than the U.S. state of New York. The population density of Syria is 284 people per square mile (110 per square km).

Syria's population growth rate was 2.13 percent in 2009. The population growth rate is the total gain of people each year, minus deaths due to childbirth and the number of people who move into a country. Syria's population growth rate is fairly high when compared to the United States at 0.98 percent,

Canada at 0.82 percent, and the European Union with a min-
iscule 0.11 percent. With the world population growth rate at
1.17 percent, Syria's rate is nearly double the global rate.

The Population Reference Bureau estimates that Syria's
population will be more than 34 million by the year 2050.
This population growth factor has many consequences for
Syrian society, including for the economy and government. For
example, think of the impact of this growth on schools, roads,
hospitals, employment, and other aspects of daily life.

Population Characteristics

How does the population of Syria break down in other ways?
One amazing statistic is that nearly 38 percent of the population is younger than 15 years of age. Thus, the middle or
median age of Syrians is a youthful 21.7 years.

The average life expectancy of Syrians from birth is 71.2
years. For men it is 69.8 years and for women it is 72.7 years.
Out of the entire population, 54 percent live in urban areas
of the country. The country also has a large rural population,
since agriculture is still very important economically for many
Syrians. In terms of gender, there are reportedly about 1.05 boys
for every girl, with this number decreasing as people age: There
are more women than men in the over-65 age group. Part of
the reason that population numbers are higher for males than
females is that not all females are reported in census data. Also,
there is a high death rate for women during childbirth.

Literacy—the ability to read and write—is not high in
Syria when compared to other countries. Nearly 80 percent
of the population is considered literate, and the rate is much
higher for men than women. While 86 percent of males are
literate, only 74 percent of women are able to read and write.
This figure is partly due to the fact that families often strictly
control women and their activities, including access to formal
education.

Within the last few decades, access to basic education has increased greatly. Under the leadership of Bashar al-Assad, the Syrian government has made large investments in building primary schools and passing measures to equip students with computer and language skills in order to make young people more competitive in the modern world. Still, education at all levels, including in rural areas and within the female population, needs to be improved.

LANGUAGE

Arabic is the official language in Syria, and it is the one that is most spoken. Still, there are other languages heard throughout the country. Kurdish areas of Syria speak Kurdish, and many Syrians speak English or French as a second language. Turks and Armenians speak their native languages in Syria, and Aramaic is still spoken by some ethnic groups.

DIET AND FOODS

Much of life in Syria revolves around the pleasure Syrians find in food and meals. Friends and family are often entertained around meals featuring local delights. The generosity of the host is often measured by the amount of food placed on the table for guests. When there is a gathering of friends or family, the men and women tend to gather separately from each other before the meal. However, all join together for the meal itself. Toasts are often offered, first by the host, followed by the guests. Much more food is offered than can be eaten, but guests would be considered rude if they did not try everything on the table. Even saying "no, thanks" can offend a generous Syrian host.

Meals for guests begin with *mezze*, which is an array of appetizers that can include pastries, pickled vegetables, dips such as hummus, raw lamb, and tabbouleh. A flat bread called *khubz* is always served with this. The khubz is used as a kind of scoop to hold the other appetizers. Tabbouleh is a mezze appetizer that includes chopped parsley, bulgur, mint, scallion, tomato, various other herbs, and lemon juice.

The main course follows the mezze and typically includes such things as lamb, chicken, skewered meats, salads, rice, casseroles, and tasty local dishes such as *maklooba* ("upside-down rice") and *moolookhiye* (flavored rice and a meat). Tea and coffee are common drinks, and fruit-flavored tobacco is frequently smoked after the meal using water pipes called *narghile*. The narghile is also common in Syrian coffee houses.

Cereal grains, especially wheat and barley, are an important part of the daily Syrian diet. Bread and pastries are very important in the life of Syrians. Many fruits and vegetables are also eaten along with meats, especially chicken in rural areas and mutton in urban areas. Foods commonly found at mealtime include tomatoes, rice, yogurt, nuts, breads, onions, and occasionally beef. Local spices tempt the taste buds and give the foods a more distinctive Syrian flavoring. The Damascus spice market provides an incredible array of fresh spices and herbs that include oregano, cumin, anise, coriander, caraway seeds, and many other wonderful flavorings.

DAILY PRACTICES AND CUSTOMS

Syria is a traditional country, and its people place great importance on traditional values. These include a strong value for
the extended family, religion, friends, education, hospitality,
courtesy, and self-discipline. Family is of primary importance.
Several generations often live in the same home, and the elderly
are highly respected. Elderly family members usually remain in
the home until death, and younger family members provide
care for the older relatives.

Marriage is an important family event. Many young
people delay getting married until they are financially stable.
However, women often marry very young, especially in rural
areas. Marriage is encouraged between members of the same
religious and ethnic groups and is still often arranged by the
family. Sometimes harsh punishments are given to those who
violate these customs. Many still practice the tradition in which
the groom pays a price, called a *mahr,* to the bride or her family
before the wedding. The mahr can be very high, even amount-
ing to several years' income. Values are slowly changing, however, as modern Syrians are having more of a role in selecting
whom they marry. Few Syrians divorce: The rate has remained
at a low 7 percent for decades.

WOMEN IN SYRIA

Although Syria has seen much progress when it comes to their
female population, new parents still tend to favor baby boys
over girls. Also, the activities of young women are carefully
scrutinized by others.

Few efforts exist in the country to advance women's rights.
As a result, women continue to suffer from laws that discriminate against them. For example, laws state that a woman may
only receive one-half of the inheritance that her husband,
brother, or male child is to receive. Syrian women are discouraged from working unless it is absolutely necessary. This situation discourages the personal, economic, and political power

that women are able to achieve in societies where women are part of the workforce.

Women's organizations in Syria estimate that more than 200 women each year are killed in "honor killings" that are carried out by a woman's family. An honor killing is the murder of a family or clan member by one or more fellow members who believe that the person has brought dishonor upon them. Although both men and women are killed in this way, women are usually the targets of this system. Many of these women were victims of rape or other forms of abuse. Yet some families persecute the victims through honor killings, which, in reality, carry little honor. One out of four married Syrian women is the victim of physical abuse. The government is beginning to crack down legally on these abuses and killings by working to protect women more effectively from these forms of violence.

Other progress in women's rights is being made: Syria elected a female vice president in 2006. Najjah Al Attar became the first Arab woman to reach such a high level of power in the Arab world. Furthermore, 14 percent of the members of Syria's parliament are women. This is also the highest in the region. The inequality in education for men and women is also narrowing as women presently make up nearly half of the university population. Although progress is being made, further efforts are still required for women to have an equal role in daily life.

RELIGION IN SYRIA

As previous chapters have discussed, Syria has many religious traditions. The country's history is filled with religious diversity. Today the country is increasingly Sunni Muslim. This section will provide a snapshot of religion in Syria.

Islam

Islam is based on the teachings of the Prophet Muhammad, the founder of the religion. Islam is based on the belief in a monotheistic (one) God. Judaism and Christianity are also monotheistic religions. Muhammad wrote the religion's basic codes of belief in Islam's most holy book, the Koran. The Koran is written in Arabic. Muhammad lived in Saudi Arabia in the seventh century, and the Koran is a compilation of writings that reflects God's teachings to Muhammad. Converts to Islam quickly spread his messages across North Africa and the Middle East, as well as into Syria, soon after Muhammad's death in 632.

The Five Pillars of Islam

Muslims around the world believe in the Five Pillars of Islam. These serve as the centerpiece practices of their faith and include the following elements:

1. The testimony of faith called *shahadah*. Believers proclaim that Allah is the one true God.

2. Prayer five times a day. Prayer takes place at dawn, noon, mid-afternoon, sunset, and at night. This ritual prayer is called *salah* and is performed facing in the direction of the city of Mecca.

3. The principle of *zakat*, which means giving support to the needy.

4. Fasting from dawn to sunset during the month of Ramadan in a practice called *sawm*.

5. A pilgrimage to Mecca, Islam's most holy city, at least once during a person's lifetime. This religious journey is called the Hajj.

The Hajj is a very important event in the life of a Muslim. It normally takes five to six days. When approaching Mecca, the religious pilgrims must change into two white cotton robes called *ihram* when they are 6.21 miles (10 km) away from the city. Upon arrival at the holy site, the pilgrims walk

Above, Islamic worshippers pray in the Masjid al-Haram Mosque on the morning of Eid-ul-Fitr day, marking the end of Ramadan during the Hajj pilgrimage in Mecca, Saudi Arabia. The Hajj is the fifth pillar of Islam and must be carried out at least once in a Muslim's lifetime, if he or she can afford to do so and is in good health.

around the Kaaba seven times. The Kaaba is Islam's most holy site and has a mosque built around it. It is a black cubical building and serves as the site toward which all Muslims pray during salah. While they circle the Kaaba, the pilgrims also touch the Black Stone seven times. Many try to kiss it seven times in their seven trips around the Kaaba. The Black Stone is located in the eastern cornerstone of the Kaaba.

Many Muslims believe that the Black Stone was sent by Allah around the time of Adam and Eve to designate a place where a sacred altar to God should be built.

For Syrian Muslims, the Hajj is one of the most important events in their life. Families plan for it many years in advance. The practice is so vital that Saudi Arabia, where the city of Mecca is located, even has a Ministry of Hajj that helps pilgrims plan their travels. Countries receive a limit to the number of their citizens who can participate in the Hajj each year.

Ramadan, the fourth pillar of Islam, is very important to devout Muslims. It takes place during the ninth month of the Islamic year, which is based on the lunar calendar. Believers fast during this period, meaning they do not take food or water from sunrise to sunset for the entire month. Fasting is practiced to cleanse the soul. Muslims are also encouraged to refrain from smoking and sexual relations. Reading the entire Koran is also encouraged during Ramadan as the time is dedicated to cultivating godliness and goodness and increasing spirituality.

Shia or Sunni?

Syria's Muslim population is 74 percent Sunni and 16 percent Shia. With Sunnis making up the vast majority of Syrians, they have a clear influence in shaping values in the country. Who are Sunni and Shia Muslims, and what are the differences between the two groups? Both groups simply refer to themselves as being Muslim, and they believe in the same Islamic beliefs and articles of faith. Still, some important differences do exist. Surprisingly, most of the differences are political and not based on religious differences.

Sunnis

Worldwide, most Muslims are Sunni. This sect believes that a Muslim can approach God directly. Shia Muslims, on the other hand, believe that communication with God requires the intervention of imams (religious leaders) or saints. Imams lead the Friday services at the mosques but do not have to be a descendant of Muhammad or his relatives. Most Sunnis believe that religious leaders should be selected on the basis of their knowledge and ability rather than their genealogy.

The word *Sunni* is derived from the Arabic word translated to mean "one who follows the traditions of the Prophet [Muhammad]." According to historical fact, Muhammad's close friend, Abu Bakr, became the first caliph of the Islamic caliphate after the Prophet's death.

Sunnis do not believe that the religious leaders should be a privileged class based on their heritage. Instead of inheriting religious power, Sunnis believe it should be earned. Sunni Muslims who are not religious leaders can even lead prayers and serve as preachers. Even with this flexibility in religious leadership, the strict practices of Islam called Wahhabism came out of a conservative sect of Sunni Islam. Extremely conservative Wahhabi teachings press for a return to fundamental Islam. These extremists look at non-Wahhabi Muslims as heretics, and some of their followers have become violent terrorists in their extremism. Osama bin Laden, for example, was raised as a Wahhabi Muslim in Saudi Arabia. Fortunately, Syria is tolerant with regard to Islam, and Wahhabism is rejected totally.

Shiite Muslims

Shia Islam is the second-largest Muslim sect in the world. Shia Muslims believe that God chose Ali ibn Abi Talib to be the caliph after the death of Muhammad. Ali was Muhammad's cousin and son-in-law and ruled over the Islamic caliphate from 656 to 661. He is believed to be the only person born in the Kaaba. Muhammad and Ali had both political and religious power during their lives, and no line was drawn between religion and government. Therefore, in some Shia Islamic countries such as Iran, religious imams are also political leaders.

The Twelve Shia is the largest of the Shia sects. Members believe that the legitimate heritage of Islam is in the family lineage of Ali ibn Abi Talib. The leaders of this lineage became 12 imams. It is from these 12 that the imams of today have descended. Shias view the imams as saints and believe that they are sinless and infallible since their teachings come directly from God. They also feel some hostility toward the companions of Muhammad whom Sunni Muslims choose to follow. Shias have a different call to prayer than the Sunnis, and many combine the five daily prayers into three each day. Shia Islam represents the majority of Muslims in a few countries, including Syria's neighbors, Lebanon, Iraq, and Iran.

Islam in Syria Today

Eighty percent of Syria's Sunni population is Arab ethnicity, with the Kurds being the second-largest group. Other Sunni ethnic groups include the Turkomans, Circassians, and Palestinians. The Sunni population cuts across all industries, professions, economic classes, social groups, and political parties. Only two of the country's provinces do not have a Sunni majority.

Although civil laws have been introduced in the country, Syria still has the remnants of two court systems. These are the civil and the traditional sharia courts. The sharia courts are religious courts based on laws found in the Koran, and they still operate in some areas of the country. They mostly work with personal issues such as marriage, divorce, child custody, and inheritance. Occasional efforts attempt to put into use a stricter version of sharia law, but the country's legal system remains mostly independent of religious law. The influences that do exist tend to discriminate against women. These include provisions related to child custody that favor the fathers. Another law permits a judge to allow a girl as young as 13 to get married. In addition, the issue that women actually cannot marry without the consent of her guardian (male relative) remains a problem (and once she marries, her husband becomes her guardian), which is a lingering result of sharia laws.

Christianity

Christians make up 10 percent of the Syrian population. The roots of the Christian population generally come from two sources. One has resulted from Western missionaries who brought the Roman Catholic and various Protestant religions to Syria. The larger Christian group has a deep history that stretches back to the earliest days of Christianity. These Christians have their heritage linked to the Eastern Orthodox Church. Even though there are many different Christian groups, they are a minority in Syria.

The Christian population in Syria is mostly located in or near the cities of Damascus, Aleppo, Hamah, and Latakia. They have a number of social characteristics that differ from the larger Muslim population. Syria's Christians tend to be better educated, more urbanized, and seldom found in low-income groups. They also tend to be better represented in professional jobs and are more active in political affairs.

Other Faiths

Smaller religious communities also exist in Syria, with groups such as the Druze, Yazidis, and even a small Jewish community. The Yazidis in Syria date back to the Umayyad caliphate in the seventh century. Most speak Kurdish, and they primarily live in Jazirah and Aleppo. Their religion combines elements of Christianity, Islam, Judaism, and paganism. They consider both the Bible and Koran to be sacred texts, but most of their faith is hidden, kept secret from outsiders.

Syria's small Jewish community is located in Damascus, Aleppo, and Al Qamishli. According to the *San Francisco Chronicle Foreign Service*, there are about 200 Jews in Syria today. Many of these communities date back to biblical times.

Syria's Jews are Arab-speaking and look like most other Arabs in the country. The government imposes some economic restrictions on the Jewish community, which is frequently spied upon by the police. Because of this persecution, many Jews have fled the country. Even the ancient Joab Ben Zeruiah Synagogue in Aleppo was closed and deserted in 1994 after 1,600 years of continuous use. Most of Syria's departing Jews have gone to either Israel or the United States.

Syria's Druze population is mainly located in the rugged mountain of the southwest in the Jebel al-Druze region and the Golan Heights. Their religion is an offshoot of Islam, but other philosophies have also been incorporated. The Druze have played an important role in the political history of Syria, as they were actively engaged in the struggle against the French. Today there are about half a million Druze in Syria.

THE ARTS

The arts in Syria thrive in both traditional and modern forms. They include many of the beautiful things that we can see and hear. Arts can be thought-provoking and also can inspire those who are exposed to them. They also reflect the soul of a society. Syria is no exception to this important factor.

Literature

Part of Syria's language history dates back more than 2,500 years to the Aramaeans. The Aramaeans simplified the Phoenician alphabet and used their language, Aramaic, to write and speak. Remnants of this language are still found in Syria near the border with Lebanon.

Today, Arabic is used to express thoughts in literature. In the tenth century, Syria was the home for Arabic poetry, but this role declined under the Ottoman Turks. Al-Mutanabbi was an Iraqi-born poet who wrote in the eleventh century. He moved to Aleppo, where he wrote much of his poetry and is considered the Syrian (and Arab) Shakespeare. Abu Firas al-Hamdan lived at the same time as al-Mutanabbi. Al-Hamdan lived in Aleppo's jail, where he wrote prison poems.

Modern Syrian literature often has a political theme, an area that for centuries was forbidden under the Ottoman Turks. Even today, authors still need to be careful in writing about contemporary political issues. Hanna Mina, Syria's most prominent novelist, is the leader in literature that describes class conflict. Historical novels are often used as a vehicle for expressing political disagreement today. Authors such as Fawwaz Haddad, Khyri al-Dhahabi, Salim Barakat, and Nabil Sulayman serve as prominent voices. Science fiction is also used at times for political dissent by authors Talib Umran and Nuhad Sharif.

Visual Arts

The Department of Fine Arts at the University of Damascus is the place where many of Syria's best artists and photographers have studied. The city continues to be the center of Syria's art scene, with many popular artists such as Abdullah Murad, whose unique abstract style has become popular around the world. Traditional Arab art is also found in Syria. Many modern artists combine classical styles with more modern elements drawn from Western art.

Music and Dance

Classical Arab music frequently has been centered in Syria. Damascus serves as a cauldron of musical creativity. Many Arab pop stars also have risen in the country, although some are now in exile so that they are freer to express themselves in their music. Syrian government censors work to rid the public media of songs that could be interpreted to be hostile to Syrian or Islamic values and customs.

Dance is also popular in Syria, but it is mostly focused upon classical and folk dance. Dabke is the national dance of Syria. The

In January 2008, Damascus celebrated the opening of festivities after it was declared Capital for Arabic Culture 2008 by the Arab culture ministers. Damascus, which has a long history of philosophers, poets, and artists, prepared for a full year of cultural activities by renovating public complexes and gardens all over Syria. Above, Syria's First Lady, Asma al-Assad, looks at a painting during the opening of the Syrian abstract art exhibition in Damascus on July 21, 2008.

term *dabke* means "stomping of the feet." The dabke takes on different forms in the various regions of Syria. Local customs and folklore serve to enhance the variations of the dance.

Film, Television, and Theater

Syria has an active Arab theater community, but it is hampered by a lack of funding. Thus, it is a hard industry in which aspiring actors and actresses can get a start. Many actors move among film, television, and theater productions. Syria is well known in the Arab world for its television soap operas. A recent phenomenon in soaps has been the use of story lines involving terrorists. These plots have been used to discourage people from engaging in these vicious practices in real life. *Bab al-Hara* is a Syrian soap opera that is based in Damascus. It is one of the most popular television programs in the Arab world. It airs during Ramadan, when families sit and watch the program together.

EDUCATION

Although literacy rates in Syria linger at about 80 percent of the population, education is now free and required for all children between the ages of 6 and 12. Nearly 5 million students are enrolled in primary and secondary schools. Only 100,000 are currently enrolled in universities, however. The country has universities in the cities of Damascus, Halab, Al Ladhiqiyah, Hims, and other cities. An online university was introduced in 2002. The Ba'ath Party used education as a propaganda tool in the 1980s, but the curriculum has improved enormously in recent years.

SPORTS

Football (or soccer, as it is called in the United States) domi-nates the sports scene in Syria. It is a sport that boys grow up dreaming about as their path to fame and fortune. The national team has not fared well in World Cup competitions, but the country's team has done well in regional tournaments. The country also has the Syrian League, which began in 1966. Here, domestic teams compete in a knockout tournament for the Syrian Cup each year.

Basketball is the second-favorite sport in Syria, but ranks a distant second behind soccer. The country has a large num-ber of club teams and leagues that compete each year. The country's national team has had little success in international competitions, but hope may be coming soon with the arrival of Wabaal Hamay. Hamay was 18 years old in 2009, a rising star at 7 feet 6 inches (229 cm).

A SNAPSHOT

It is difficult to capture the culture and life of any country's people in a few pages. This chapter has taken a snapshot of the daily life and society in Syria. It has provided a look at key cultural elements and how they contribute to the complexity of Syria's people. This snapshot has also shown that Syrians, like most people in the world, value friends and family and are welcoming to guests. The next chapter will show how Syria is governed, another key element in understanding the complexity of the nation.

CHAPTER

6

Government and Politics

An examination of Syria's history shows that its governance has been filled with political turmoil, twists, and turns. Outsiders ruled for thousands of years, with many of the world's great civilizations governing the area much of the time prior to the twentieth century. The twentieth century brought a change, but it brought a dictatorship instead of democracy. An examination of Syria's government is therefore not a story of democratic successes and citizen rights.

Syria today is a state with a government that is much different from those found in democratic societies. Instead of many political parties competing for power, the country's 1973 constitution bestows great power to the Ba'ath Party. In reality, Syria is a country in which the Ba'ath Party maintains a tightly controlled dictatorship. It uses the military and the party to control government, social, and economic affairs. Yet, although the Ba'ath Party is the controlling force in Syrian government, it is not the only political party. Other parties remain secondary in public affairs and continue to exist in minor roles.

The country has had a father and son lead the country, with Hafez al-Assad serving as president from 1971 to 2000 and his son, Bashar al-Assad, serving in the presidency from 2000 until the present. With the death of Hafez al-Assad in June 2000, Syria's parliament changed the country's constitution to allow Bashar to become president. At the time, Bashar was too young, so the age requirement for the presidency was lowered from 40 to 34.

Bashar had little interest in politics. In fact, his father had once favored another son, Basil, to follow him as president. However, Basil died in 1994 in a car accident. Thus, Bashar was recruited by the Ba'ath Party and elected with over 97 percent of the vote in July 2000. He was reelected president in 2007.

It is important to examine many elements in order to understand Syria's government today. These elements include the constitution, the three branches of government, the Ba'ath Party, local governments, the role of the military, and the roles of the citizen.

THE CONSTITUTION

Constitutions are the foundation of a country's government. These important documents establish governmental bodies and identify their responsibilities. They also identify and protect the rights of citizens. In many societies, all people are subject to the laws of the country, even the leaders. This is called "rule of law." When some people are above the law and not held responsible for any crimes committed, a society has what is called the "rule of man." This means that some in the society operate beyond the laws and will not be held accountable for violating them or the rights of other citizens.

In 2007, hundreds of thousands of Syrian citizens filled the main square in Damascus to celebrate the reelection of President Bashar al-Assad to a second term. Al-Assad was the sole candidate for the presidency. The demonstrators held banners with al-Assad's image and posters that read, "We all love you."

Sadly, the rule of man is more the case in Syria's government. A prime example of this was the constitutional age requirement to be president. As has already been explained, the Syrian legislative body simply changed the law to accommodate Bashar al-Assad's age of 34.

BRANCHES OF GOVERNMENT

The 1973 constitution established the three branches of government that include the legislative, executive, and judicial. The constitution also outlines the voting rights of citizens, along with the working procedures of the branches of government. The power given to the Ba'ath Party is also included in the constitution's opening section, as well as in Article 8. It states: "The leading party in the society and the state is the Socialist Arab Ba'ath Party. It leads a patriotic and progressive front seeking to unify the resources of the people's masses and place them at the service of the Arab nation's goals." Thus, the constitution sanctions the primary role of the Ba'ath Party in the country's governance.

Legislative Branch

The legislative branch is responsible for making laws in the country. In Syria, the legislative branch has one house that is called the People's Council. A one-house legislature is referred to as unicameral, while governments with two houses like Canada or the United States are bicameral, with two houses.

The People's Council has 250 members who each serve four-year terms. The last elections were held in April 2007, and the next elections are slated for 2011. Voters must be at least 18 years of age and must meet the requirements of Syrian election laws. These provisions guarantee the freedom of voters in electing their representatives; the integrity of the election; the right of the candidates to watch over the voting; and punishment for those who tamper with the will of the voters. The council meets at least three times a year and in special sessions called by the president of the council or the country's president. The president of the People's Council presides over the body and is the public voice for the council's interests. The constitution stipulates that at least half of the council seats are set aside for "workers and peasants."

Council powers include nominating the president; approval of the budget, treaties, and development planning; and the ratification of treaties. The body may also act on a motion of no confidence from cabinet members and ministers. This suggests a lack of faith in the current government, and those members who receive the no confidence vote must resign. In all, the legislative branch in Syria is quite weak. Most power is placed in the Ba'ath Party and in the executive branch.

Executive Branch

Syria's executive branch has been dominated by presidents Hafez and Bashar al-Assad since the constitution was put in place. The president is elected for a term of seven years and heads the executive branch in Syria. A vice president assumes the presidency if the office becomes vacant. The constitution requires that the president be a Muslim and an Arab Syrian. The Ba'ath Party proposes the presidential candidate to the People's Council. Upon approval by the council, the presidential nominee must receive at least a majority of the votes of citizens. The citizens have little choice, though, as Bashar al-Assad was the only candidate listed on the ballot in the 2000 and 2007 elections.

Great powers are placed in the presidency. For one, the president appoints vice presidents, high court justices, the prime minister, and other ministers. The president also calls cabinet meetings. The president can veto laws, issue decrees, declare war, conduct foreign policy, declare a state of emergency, and ratify treaties. The president is commander in chief of the military and can award honors and decorations to individuals. In all, the office of the presidency is very strong when compared to executives in democratic nations where the power of the office is subject to greater limitations.

Judicial Branch

The Supreme Constitutional Court is the highest court in Syria. Its justices are appointed by the president for four-year terms. The court has four justices and a fifth who serves as the chief justice. The court rules on whether or not laws are constitutional, as well as on other issues such as election disputes. It is clear from the constitution that the president can go around the highest court in a number of ways. This means that the president, in reality, cannot be held accountable by the court or the constitution.

Lower-level courts include the Court of Cassation and Appeals Courts. The Court of Cassation is higher than the Appeals Courts and can rule on the decisions of the lower courts. Governorates (states) have courts called Tribunals of First Instance. These courts hear civil and criminal cases. Tribunals of Peace hear minor cases at the local level, while Personal Status Courts hear cases on family matters and personal issues.

THE BA'ATH PARTY

The Arab Socialist Ba'ath Party was founded in Damascus in 1947. The party pursued a socialist economic path, Arab freedom, and an anti-colonial stance along with other Arab groups in the Middle East. The party violently swept into power in Syria in 1963 and has held the political reign since then. The Arabic word *Ba'ath* means "resurrection" or "renaissance," and the party is the leading one in the seven political parties that form the National Progressive Front (NPF). The NPF is the coalition that controls three-fourths of the seats in the People's Congress. The Syrian Ba'ath Party also has branches in other Middle Eastern countries such as Lebanon, Iraq, and Jordan.

LOCAL GOVERNMENTS

Syria has many governments beyond the national level. The country has 14 governorates, which are much like U.S. states or Canadian provinces. The governorates are headed by a governor who is appointed by Syria's interior minister. Each governorate has a provincial council, three-quarters of whose members are elected by its citizens. The remainder are appointed by the minister of the interior and the governor.

The governorates are divided into 60 districts. Districts are divided further into 206 sub-districts. The districts and sub-districts are governed by officials who are appointed by the governor. These individuals work with district and sub-district councils that are elected. The district and sub-district officials are responsible for local issues and needs as well as serving as a channel to higher levels of government.

THE ARMED FORCES

The military plays an important part in the life of Syria. Under the power of the president, who is its commander in chief, the military can also be used as a political tool to control the country's population. Syria has about 400,000 people in its military, with half of these serving in the reserves. The Syrian Armed Forces are headquartered in Damascus and include an army, navy, air force, air defense force, and a police and security force.

Upon reaching the age of 18, young men are conscripted to serve 24 months in the military. Conscription means that it is required for young men to serve.

Syria also has long been in disagreement with the United States, Israel, and others in the region. Sometimes it is because of interference in places such as Lebanon and because of Syria's hostile attitude toward Israel. Syria also possesses stockpiles of biological and chemical weapons that serve to threaten nearby countries. The country claims that these weapons serve to discourage Israel from attacking. Reports in 2007 indicated that Israel bombed a nuclear reactor site in Syria. Tensions between these two nations continue to fester, with Syria refusing to recognize the state of Israel.

The military also has been used to control problems within Syria. For example, in 1980 the military put an end to an uprising by the Muslim Brotherhood (a group who undertook guerrilla activities targeting government officials) in the country. Over the years, both Hafez and Bashar al-Assad made the army

Syrian-Lebanese relations are complex, due to the Syrian political pressure and military presence in Lebanon from 1975 to 2005. In fact, Syria has only recently recognized Lebanon as a sovereign country, although Lebanon gained its independence in 1942. Above, Syrian troops, deployed to combat smuggling and arrest fugitives along the Syrian-Lebanese border in the eastern Bekaa region, are seen at an observation point in October 2008.

their personal tool for asserting control over the population. The military continues to be used by the president to protect his international and domestic interests. The situation for citizens has indeed improved under Bashar. Still, there is a distance to go for citizens seeking freedom and constitutional rights.

THE ROLES OF THE CITIZEN

Syria's citizens have rights and responsibilities listed in the consti-tution. However, since Syria works under the rule of man instead of the rule of law, these rights are frequently not protected. The international human rights organization Amnesty International cites several issues that are problems for citizens in Syria: crackdowns on protests, the killing of civilians, the use of torture, and a lack of freedom of expression. This means that citizens who actually choose to exercise their rights—such as the freedom of expression—may be severely punished. The constitution's protections have little value in a dictatorship.

The constitution actually protects most of the areas mentioned as problems by Amnesty International, but these rights are not being equally enforced. The following is a list of some of the rights mentioned in the constitution:

- Freedom of expression

- Equality of opportunity

- Right to participate in government

- Presumption of innocence in courts

- Protection from torture

- Privacy

- Freedom of faith

- Right to work

- Right to assemble in groups and protest

- Right to an education

In addition to the rights found in the constitution, some duties and responsibilities are required of citizens. These include the duty to work, pay taxes, preserve national unity, and defend the homeland.

TWENTY-FIRST-CENTURY FOREIGN AFFAIRS

With the Ba'ath Party and the al-Assad family ruling Syria for nearly four decades, the country remains a dictatorship. Efforts to protest for democracy are put down by the government. New talks between Syria and Israel that started in 2008 may improve the relationship between the two countries. This would provide an important step following Israel's successful agreements with Egypt and Jordan, which have aided in promoting peace in the Middle East.

The election of Barack Obama as president of the United States ushered in new attempts at cooling off the longtime hostility between Syria and the United States. Bashar al-Assad has shown increased interest in becoming friendlier with the United States and other Western countries. This change, combined with a softer hand in domestic affairs, may mean that the country is starting to move toward greater protections of the rights of citizens. Bashar's leadership has remained less harsh than his father's rule. This brings hope to many within Syria and around the world.

CHAPTER

7

Syria's
Economy

Economic activity is the lifeblood of societies. The better this economic lifeblood operates in a country, the better off its citizens will be. They will have jobs and many other social services and opportunities that allow them to prosper and to enjoy life.

What contributes to an effective economy? A number of factors play a role, including the role of the government in the economy, openness and truth in businesses and government, natural resources, the amount of money available, and the quality of the workforce. Factors that contribute to a high-quality workforce include education, work ethic and personal responsibility, creativity, and management skills. The role of women also plays an important factor in the workforce. Sometimes, however, religion or other cultural practices discourage women from working outside of the home.

Economic power is important to a country because it allows the nation to defend itself, provide for its people, and create prosperity. Syria's past has shown that it was once a crossroads of land travel between Asia, Africa, and Europe. This advantageous location provided early Syrians with knowledge, trade, and new technologies. It also brought in many outside rulers, as has been seen in earlier chapters. Damascus has long served as the center for Syria's political and economic activity. This pattern continues today, with the bustling city at the hub of Syria's economy.

Countries also can suffer from government involvement in the economy. This has happened in Syria, where the government has exercised inefficient and corrupt central control of the economy. These factors and a lack of honesty and openness have made Syrians and potential outside investors wary of the political environment for economic development.

THE TWIN FOUNDATIONS OF SYRIA'S ECONOMY

Two elements provide the foundation for Syria's economy today. These are the agriculture and petroleum sectors, which make up half of the country's gross domestic product (GDP). A country's GDP is the total value of the goods and services produced within a country in a year. Syria's GDP in 2008 was 44.49 billion U.S. dollars.

Agriculture

Agriculture is vital to Syria's economy. The ancient waters of the Euphrates River and its tributaries have nourished crops for millennia. Other rivers, including the Orontes (Syria's second-longest river) and the Barrada, are also important in supporting the country's agricultural industry. One-fifth of the agricultural lands are irrigated, but production could be increased with additional irrigation. The problem in these areas is that, although there is an adequate amount of rain received there, in the coastal Mediterranean climate, the rainy season is during the winter and not during the growing season.

The crops Syria produces are varied and include two major grains—wheat and barley—along with other products such as cotton, sugar beets, grapes, olives, citrus fruits, lentils, chick-peas, and vegetables. Animal products include eggs, beef, mutton, poultry, milk, and chevon (goat meat). Cotton was once the most important export in the country, until it was replaced by petroleum in the 1970s.

Farming practices in Syria continue to be inefficient in terms of production. Many factors contribute to this inefficiency, including poor soil conditions, which are not corrected by adequate use of fertilizers. Farmers also fail to rotate crops, leading to further degradation of the soil. When farmers rotate crops, they grow a variety of crops in the same area in sequential seasons in order to avoid the buildup of biological agents and pests that occur when one species is continually cropped. Lack of adequate water continues to plague agriculture, along with frequent missteps by the government in past years. Increasing the amount of land available for agricultural use is also difficult, because one-fifth of the country is desert. This, combined with the growth of cities and roads, continues to take land out of agricultural use at a rate nearly equal to that of new farming lands brought into production.

Of the country's entire labor force, 42 percent is engaged in agriculture. (As a comparison, the figure for the United States is under 1 percent.) Thus, nearly half of all Syrians are dependent upon agriculture for their economic survival. Cotton, wheat, fruits, vegetables, and meats are exported by Syria, but the country also continues to import various food products.

Petroleum

Oil was discovered in northeast Syria in the 1950s. The industry blossomed into a vibrant part of the economy by the 1970s.

The Euphrates Valley, where the women above are working in the fields, has had a rich, fertile agricultural history. Since biblical times, the land in Syria has supported the country's economy. However, because of modern farming equipment, industrial expansion, and population growth, many of its wetlands have been drained for irrigation purposes.

With reserves much smaller than nearby oil producers such as Saudi Arabia, Iran, and Iraq, Syria's production started to decrease by the mid-1990s. Today, it is predicted that Syria will become an importer of oil by 2012 as their present fields rapidly dwindle in production. Petroleum provided a major boost to Syria's economy in the late twentieth century, but it will soon need to be replaced.

In addition to oil, Syria produces natural gas. Presently, the country's natural gas is used domestically, but plans are being developed to export it in the future. In 2008, Syria ranked forty-second in the world in terms of proven natural gas reserves.

Syria faces a major looming economic problem as one of its economic foundations, the petroleum industry, falters due to decreasing production. What will replace this element in the economy? This question will be explored later in this chapter.

OTHER BRANCHES OF THE ECONOMY

Elements other than agriculture and oil also contribute to Syria's economy. These include a variety of manufacturing and a number of services, including banking, government, and a growing tourism industry. Government employment currently makes up more than 25 percent of the jobs in the country.

The government's hand in many areas of the economy has been laced with corruption that makes trade more difficult. Industries such as banking and manufacturing were taken over by the government and have suffered as private enterprise was lacking in the country. During the 1990s, private businesses were allowed to develop. Starting in 2002, the country allowed private banks to operate. These elements have added to the strength of the Syrian economy. If allowed to grow with little government interference, they promise more opportunities for future jobs.

The government's declining role in the economy has also included a decrease in subsidies for some products. Most notable among these are gas and cement, for which prices have been allowed to rise closer to actual market values. Government subsidies had kept these products artificially cheap before these changes. Some goods and services continue to be subsidized by the government. These include diesel fuel and various social services. The ability of the government to continue subsidizing services and diesel fuel is decreasing because of less oil money fueling the government. This means that the government will need to either decrease its reach, or to increase its revenue sources. These are problems that are not easily solved.

Tourism

Tourism is an area of increasing economic opportunity in Syria. Blessed with fantastic historical sites and a fascinating culture, the country provides an inviting array of attractions for visitors. For example, the cities of Damascus, Aleppo, and Bosra and the ancient ruins of Palmyra are all listed as United Nations Educational, Scientific and Cultural Organization (UNESCO) World Heritage sites. Some of these sites will be discussed further in Chapter 8. The country is open to tourists, and even Americans are welcomed. This is perhaps surprising, considering the hostility that marked the relations between the two countries in the early twenty-first century. The stark exception is that Israelis are not welcomed. Even travelers with an Israeli stamp in their passport are denied entry to Syria.

A factor discouraging tourism has been the shady reputation of the Syrian government and its questionable involvement in Lebanon, Palestine, and Iraq. These actions have offended or frightened many potential visitors in the international community. Some in the United States and other Western societies still portray Syria as a dangerous place populated by terrorists and radical Muslim extremists. To the contrary, the Syrian people are very friendly, welcoming, and hospitable to visitors.

Between April 2008 and April 2009, tourist numbers increased by 19 percent. Most of the increases are due to more Arab tourists, many of whom are traveling to religious sites in Syria. However, the same time period also saw European visitors increasing by a whopping 54 percent, with many new visitors from Germany and Italy. Revenue from tourism produced 1.1 billion U.S. dollars in the first four months of 2009. The Ministry of Tourism credited the increase to advertising in European and Arab nations. This success is encouraging the Ministry of Tourism to conduct a global tourism campaign to attract more visitors and revenue for the country's economy. Lingering tourism problems include the lack of airlines that serve Syria and inadequate development of entertainment and cultural programs for visitors.

Manufacturing

One-eighth of the Syrian economy, or about 13 percent, is based upon manufacturing. This area has not been a traditional strength, but it still contributes to diversifying the country's economy. Major industries besides petroleum include textiles, food, sugar, beverages, tobacco, car assembly, chemicals, steel, cement, and building materials. Cement and building materials have been run by the state, while private industries are on the rise in the areas of textiles, paper, leather, foods, sugar processing, and other manufacturing. Some of these industries also have government ownership, such as textiles, which has been quite profitable under state management. Traditionally, the textile industry has been the country's largest manufacturing industry other than oil. Making yarn out of the country's cotton has been a major segment of the textile industry.

Syria continues to reach out to other nations for investments that will expand its manufacturing. Saudi Arabia and other Arab nations have been most supportive and continue to subsidize Syrian energy consumption. This is vital to developing the manufacturing sector. The United States also indicated in 2009 that it might begin loosening the economic sanctions placed on Syria. This could also enhance foreign investment.

Mining

Petroleum products are not Syria's only source of resource wealth. Many other minerals are found in enough quantities for profitable mining. These include phosphate rock, salt, limestone, gypsum, sandstone, and asphalt. Phosphates are used to make fertilizer, and sandstone is used to manufacture glass. Other minerals such as gold, lead, iron ore, copper, and coal are found in the mountain areas, but most are not plentiful enough for mining projects.

Financial Services

The government's traditional grip on the banking and financial services has limited this sector of the economy. Prior to 2001, the government would not lend money to private businesses. As a result, these financial (and other) businesses were slow to grow outside of government control. Foreign investment helped somewhat, but the country's tainted political record limited these efforts mainly to Arab investors. With the legalization of private banking in 2001, the industry has grown rapidly. Nonetheless, it remains somewhat inefficient, with the main difficulty being the inability to obtain outside investments.

Reform is slowly happening in Syria in the financial sector. Private money exchangers were allowed in 2007 for the first time, and private stock brokerage firms have been permitted. Syria's first stock market in 40 years was opened in 2009 with a handful of companies being traded. This effort demonstrates the country's interest in expanding the range of economic activities in the economy, although the transition from government involvement, control, and intervention has been slow. The new stock exchange, centered in Damascus, may provide opportunities for private Syrian companies to obtain investments necessary to expand their business and the private sector. The ability to gain investors in the Syrian stock market will receive an important boost if the political atmosphere between Syria and the United States improves. Saudi Arabia is another major investor in the Middle East. Its relations with the Syrians promised other positive economic breakthroughs in 2009.

Energy

Syria produces and uses mostly thermal and hydroelectric power. Thermal power provides about two-thirds of the country's electricity, and hydroelectric supplies the other third. Thermal power is primarily generated by the use of oil-fueled plants. Hydroelectric power is also very important and is mostly generated by the Euphrates River Plant. The country is self-sufficient for its power needs, but this situation may change in the future as the population increases and domestic oil supplies decrease. Electricity problems include inefficiency and periodic power outages.

Communication Systems

Communication systems provide necessary links among people and to information. Communication systems include telephone, radio, television, Internet, newspapers, mail, and magazines. All of these systems are in use in Syria. The country has 3.6 million land phone lines and 7 million cell phones. The total suggests that there is nearly one phone for every two Syrians. The country also has 44 television stations, 16 radio stations, and nearly 3.5 million Internet users (about 17 percent of the population). Syria's Internet country code is *.sy*.

The quality of communications is rapidly improving with the addition of new technology, microwave relay networks, and two satellite earth stations positioned over the Indian Ocean. However, these improvements have moved at a slower pace than in other countries because Western nations have blocked trading technology to Syria.

The government and Ba'ath Party control and own much of the media in Syria. This greatly limits freedom of expression in newspapers and on television and radio. Government censorship and author self-censorship are regular practices. Criticism of the president is forbidden. Some improvement has taken place since the election of Bashar al-Assad, but problems still exist, especially for the foreign media, which are tightly

Because television, audio, and print media are government run, Syrian journalism has become known for its pieces praising government policy and government leaders. A number of people working in the media, in fact, have been hired because of their connections to those in power. Those in the media who oppose government policy risk losing their jobs, censorship, or imprisonment. Above, journalists work in the media center for the Arab Summit in Damascus in March 2008.

controlled in the country. A media watchdog organization called Reporters Without Borders has branded Syria as one of the worst offenders against freedom of information. The country regularly censors opposing points of view and bans independent news Web sites.

Transportation

Efficient transportation systems contribute mightily to a country's prosperity. Quality roads, railways, waterways, pipelines, and air and shipping systems all contribute to moving people and goods from one place to another in a well-organized manner. These systems, combined with modern transportation technology, can make a country's economy much more proficient. In Syria, however, the bulk of goods and people are carried, carted, bused, or trucked on the roads of the country.

Syria has 60,522 miles (97,401 km) of roadway, and 12,110 miles (19,490 km) of these roads are paved. Trains operate on 1,684 miles (2,711 km) of railroad track. Rail also connects Syria to Iraq, Jordan, and Turkey. Damascus serves as the main center for the country's road, rail, and air transportation networks. More than 3 million travelers annually go through Damascus International Airport, with the number increasing each year. Although international service is limited, a traveler can still take direct flights to and from Damascus and Moscow, London, Istanbul, Dubai, Prague, Cairo, Khartoum, Caracas, Vienna, Tehran, Amman, and a few other cities. Syria's national airline has been hampered in recent years by the trade prohibitions on technical parts imposed by the United States and others countries. This has made it difficult for Syria to obtain replacement parts for its airline.

With the petroleum industry's importance, pipelines move crude oil and other petroleum products across the country. Shipping from the port cities of Baniyas, Jablah, Latakia, and Tartus serve as important links on the Mediterranean Sea that provide for trade with other nations.

Foreign Trade

Syria's location was a prime factor for centuries in the region's trade with other areas of the world. When land transportation ruled, Syria benefited. However, with the rise of ships, canals, and airplanes, Syria's role as an intersection of trade was severely diminished. This, combined with political problems between the Ba'athist regime and much of the rest of the world, has hampered the country's modern development as a trading nation.

Most of the country's trade today is with fellow Arab nations in the region. Syria imports about 160,000 barrels of oil per day from others in the region. This number increases each year. Other imports include machinery and transportation vehicles, food, plastics, livestock, and other products. The country exported crude oil for the first decade of the twenty-first century, along with textiles, cotton, clothing, minerals, wheat, fruits, vegetables, and petroleum products. Syria's primary imports are drawn from Saudi Arabia (oil), China, Egypt, Italy, the United Arab Emirates (UAE), Ukraine, Russia, Germany, and Iran. Syria exports most of its goods to Iraq, Lebanon, Germany, Italy, Egypt, Saudi Arabia, and France. Syria has a trade free zone with Iraq; this war-torn country took 30 percent of Syria's total exports in 2007, and the amount increases annually.

Syria's continuing conflict with Israel has also isolated the country from many important international trade agreements. For example, the country withdrew from the General Agreement on Tariffs and Trade (GATT) in 1951 when Israel was admitted to the international agreement. This agreement was replaced by the World Trade Organization (WTO) in 1995, which, as of the writing of this book, Syria had not joined. However, this situation may be changing in the near future. The country started the process to join the WTO shortly after Bashar al-Assad assumed the presidency.

Syria does belong to the new regional trade association called the Greater Arab Free Trade Area (GAFTA), which began in 2005. This organization eliminated duties on goods moving among GAFTA member countries. Syria also has a free trade agreement with the neighboring country of Turkey.

THE HUMAN SIDE OF THE ECONOMY

The impact of the economy on the people of Syria is also important to investigate. Economic data tell us the following about the economic status of Syrians:

1. More than 5.5 million Syrians are in the country's workforce.

2. The per capita GDP is estimated at 4,800 U.S. dollars in 2008, ranking it 144th in the world.

3. Unemployment was 9 percent in 2008.

4. Nearly 12 percent of the population falls below the poverty level.

5. Inflation was 14.9 percent in 2008.

Statistics provide cold, hard data about the economy and its impact on the people of Syria, but they do not tell the human story. The high inflation rate and low per capita GDP mean that life is difficult and often only the basic needs of people are met. The unemployment rate was near that of the United States in 2009, which leaves many wanting to work but not able to get a job. Thousands of families are impacted by the lack of jobs, one result of which is a high rate of poverty. New efforts to decrease government control of the economy and increase private business are vitally important for improving the daily lives of Syrians.

LOOKING AHEAD

Syria appears to be poised on the brink of significant economic advancement. This observation is based upon the recent increase in private businesses and banking and the decreasing role of government. Although this transition has been painfully slow for many Syrians, it does appear to be moving forward on both the home and international fronts. The huge problem of replacing the country's oil money in the economy has created the need for change. At the same time, the rise of President Bashar al-Assad has loosened the government's reins on the economy.

If Syria's government decides to participate more in the international community and warms relations with the United States and other Western countries, new opportunities will blossom. U.S. president Barack Obama has extended a hand to Syria that presents great potential. Improvement in the relations between Syria and Israel can further enhance the country's role in the region and the world in terms of economic and political influence. Syrians are watching closely and hope that their country's economic lifeblood flows toward a much more prosperous future.

CHAPTER

8

Living in Syria Today

A ny book discussing Syria would be lacking if it did not spend some time discussing the country's amazing sights and cities. Syria's lengthy history has made possible some incredible places for residents and visitors alike. Located at the continental crossroads, the country has been fortunate to have sites today that reflect the best of Syria's journey though time.

More than half of all Syrians live in urban areas. While Damascus is the country's urban crown jewel, there are other cities that are also very important. This section describes important aspects of key cities in Syria and some of the factors that make each city special.

ALEPPO

Aleppo is a city in northeast Syria with a population of more than 4 million people in the immediate area. The city dates to the eleventh century B.C., meaning it has existed for more than 3,000 years. This makes it one of the world's oldest cities. Aleppo has an advantageous location midway between the Mediterranean Sea and the Euphrates River. The city was also located on a prime route from Damascus to Ankara, Turkey, and beyond to India. The city's location on the Silk Road and between important bodies of water was of key importance in its history. As a result of its location, the city was one of the country's first to develop railroad lines that linked the Aleppo ports and other cities. This provided an important economic benefit that still exists today, as Aleppo is the headquarters of Syria's national railway system.

Aleppo was devastated in 1138 when an earthquake struck. Nearly a quarter of a million people are believed to have died in the earthquake. This is the fourth-worst recorded earthquake in the history of the world. Many important battles have also taken place in Aleppo over thousands of years. Remnants of these struggles lay buried beneath the city. Aleppo sprawls over these remnants and other vast archeological sites, many of which remain undiscovered.

Aleppo International Airport connects the city to many places in Europe, North Africa, and the Middle East. Thus, cities such as London, Bahrain, Cairo, Amman, and Istanbul are only a flight away.

Despite being at the intersection of trade for centuries, Aleppo's importance as a major trading center has declined over the past century. Today the city is a hub for agricultural activity. Wheat, cotton, sheep, olives, and other products are grown in the area around the city. A visitor will be surprised to see modern transportation mixed with horse- and donkey-drawn carts.

Aleppo is really two cities, one old, the other new. The old city is ancient and was once surrounded by walls. The new city has grown up around the old city. A key feature of the old city is the Citadel, an immense medieval castle located on a hill in

When the Ottoman Empire built the Baghdad Railway through the city of Aleppo in 1912, it became the first city in Syria to have railway connection. Today, Aleppo is the headquarters for the country's national railway network, Chemins de Fer Syriens.

the city center. The Citadel was built in the thirteenth century. Construction of the Great Mosque of Aleppo was started in 1158. It is the oldest mosque in Aleppo. This mosque is said to be the site where John the Baptist's father, Zechariah, is buried. (It was John the Baptist who baptized Jesus.) The mosque was renovated in 2003 and is still used today.

LATAKIA

Latakia is Syria's busiest seaport. It is located in the northwest section of the country on the Mediterranean Sea. With a population of more than 350,000 and a history that goes back three millennia, Latakia is a busy and fascinating city. Its past has been influenced and controlled at times by the Phoenicians,

Canaanites, Romans, Seleucids, Byzantines, Arabs, Seljuks, Crusaders, Mamluks, and the Ottoman Turks. The city is even mentioned in the Bible in Revelations and in Paul's letter to the Colossians. Thus, the multiple influences of trade, religion, and foreign invaders make the city a holder of many amazing stories.

The city's natural port provides a solid foundation for the local economy. Many containers move through the port as agricultural products from inland are exported. Amazing as it may seem, this port has been used continuously for more than 3,000 years. An additional important source of income is the money that expatriates send back to relatives living in the city.

Tourism is of rising importance to Latakia. Many resorts have sprung up along the coast and tempt visitors to retreat to the warm, sandy Mediterranean beaches. Many visitors also come to participate in Latakia's Flower Festival each year in April and the Festival of Love and Peace in early August. Because of the frequent contact with foreigners through trade and tourism, Latakia has become one of Syria's most liberal places. These outside influences have kept the city and its residents looking outward and forward in many ways. For example, many young women wear jeans and colorful tops instead of more traditional Muslim attire.

HIMS

Hims is Syria's third-largest city, with nearly 900,000 residents. The city boasts a strong agricultural and industrial economic base that produces wheat, sugar beets, cotton, barley, and a host of other farming products. The industrial foundations include an oil refinery, fertilizer plant, sugar refinery, and an automobile plant.

Tourism supplements the industrial and agricultural parts of the economy. Many important historical sites are located near the city. These include Krak des Chevaliers, a stunning UNESCO World Heritage Site. Krak des Chevaliers is a medieval Crusader fortress located only 25 miles (40 km) from the city. Another attraction is nearby Marmarita, a popular summer destination.

The city is located in west-central Syria near the Lebanon border. Like Aleppo and Damascus, it has an old city. Its founding was before the birth of Christ, and it served as a place that protected inner Syria from invading forces. It also was subject to bombing during the Yom Kippur War with Israel in 1973, when its refinery was attacked.

Today Hims hosts the Desert Folk Festival during the first week of May. This event is highlighted by the city's closeness to the Syrian Desert, which begins just to the east of Hims. The event is marked by elaborate desert costumes and clothing and by events such as camel, horse, and car races. The city is also the home of two football (soccer) teams, including the eight-time Syrian Cup champion team the Al-Karamah Blue Adlers.

DAMASCUS

Earlier chapters have chronicled parts of the story about Damascus, which is one of the great cities of the world. It has an enviable past packed with historic events and people. This history dates from the ancient civilization at Tell Ramad, located on the outskirts of the city, dating back 12,000 to 13,000 years. Damascus is the source of both Christian and Islamic roots. It claims to have the longest history of continuous inhabitance of any city in the world. And it has fallen to many of the greatest conquerors and empires the world has ever known. As U.S. author and humorist Mark Twain said in *The Innocents Abroad*: ". . . there was always a Damascus . . . she has looked upon the dry bones of a thousand empires and will see the tombs of a thousand more before she dies." Simply stated, a visitor who goes to Syria and misses Damascus would be missing the heart of the country's story.

Visitors from Syria, the Middle East, and the rest of the world flock to Damascus for its unparalleled history, bazaars, old winding alleys and streets, mosques, food, coffeehouses, and stories. With nearly 5 million people living in the city and surrounding area, Damascus is Syria's hub for economic, social, and cultural life. A spectacular introduction to Damascus is available by seeing a panoramic view of the city from Mount Qasioun.

The two major sections of Damascus are the Old City and the surrounding city. The Old City is a UNESCO World Heritage Site that is walled and contains captivating markets, mosques, streets, minarets, and shrines. A key feature is the Umayyad Mosque, which is Syria's most important religious building and one of the oldest mosques in the world. The mosque is considered the fourth-most holy in the world. It claims to hold the head of John the Baptist, who is revered as a prophet by both Muslims and Christians. Other key sites in the Old City are the Citadel of Damascus, St. Paul's Chapel, and the shrine to Saladin. Challenges face Damascus as the encroaching city with its pollution and increasing population are now endangering some of the Old City sites and activities.

Modern Damascus sprawls out from the Old City and serves as the modern face of Syria. The international airport and bus station serve as hubs for transportation to the rest of the country and to other countries. Television, newspaper, and other national media also are centered in Damascus. Amazing restaurants, Turkish baths, museums, art galleries, and the bustling city's social life are available for visitors in the newer sections of the city.

PALMYRA

Located 133 miles (215 km) northeast of Damascus is the ancient city of Palmyra, another UNESCO World Heritage Site. This city is a jewel in Syria's crown that possesses the ancient ruins of a once-great city. In earlier times this location served as a caravan city for people venturing across the Syrian Desert. The trading route through the city linked the ports on the

Damascus is the oldest continuously inhabited city in the world. The city has a wealth of historical sites but is also a modern city, home to many sports clubs, cafes, and malls.

Mediterranean Sea with Persia. The Roman Emperor Hadrian even visited Palmyra in A.D. 129 and declared it a free city. Today it is a must-see location for tourists.

Among the ancient ruins in Palmyra, called Tadmor in Hebrew, was a temple that is attributed to Solomon and was built some 4,000 years ago. Important structures in the ruins today include the Temple of Bel. This ancient structure was considered to be the most significant religious site in Syria in the time period right after the birth of Christ. Other key structures include the Tower tomb, an inscription of Queen Zenobia on a column, the well-preserved theater, and the lengthy stretch of columns on the *decumanus,* which was the main street. These features become even more amazing for visitors in the light hues at dawn or at sunset. Nearby is the Valley of the Tombs, which includes the remains of Romans whose grave sites are marked with beautiful limestone bust sculptures.

Around the historic city of Palmyra, a modern city has arisen. Modern Palmyra is a city of 50,000 people and, not surprisingly, tourism is the main industry. Unfortunately, the tourism industry weakened after the September 11, 2001, terrorist attacks in the United States. Cutthroat competition between tourism businesses in Palmyra further deepened the damage of the attack, as profits shrank and hostility grew among the businesses and people. Visitors today will find an incredible historical site at Palmyra that is not very busy with visitors. This allows guests to wander at their leisure to explore the remarkable sites at Palmyra.

SYRIAN SITES

Syria has many amazing sites because of its important location and because of a long and complex history. With the many outsiders who passed through the land, other cultures contributed greatly to the architecture and development of Syria. The following sites are located in or near smaller villages and hold great historic importance. They are places that visitors will want to see if they are in the area, as they predate most of the history found in North America, South America, and Australia. Here are a few of Syria's other treasures.

Bosra

Bosra was once a busy city with more than 80,000 residents. Today, however, it is only a village with a remarkable heritage. Located in southern Syria near the border with Jordan, it is a city that lies in ruins that show evidence of a once great culture and society. Bosra was once the Nabatean capital and later served as the capital of the Roman province of Arabia starting in 106. The city's history dates back to 1300 B.C., when it was mentioned in ancient Egyptian records. Later, a young Muhammad met an influential Christian monk named Bahira in Bosra. Bahira revealed to Muhammad's uncle Abu Talib that Muhammad would be the Prophet.

Sites here include a spectacular Roman theater that is very well preserved within the walls of the citadel. Seats are stepped so spectators could see the performances on the stage at the center of the crescent-shaped theater. An audience of 9,000 people could attend the performances—a huge audience for that time period. Performances are still held in the theater today. The Bosra Festival is held every other year on odd-numbered years. Other ruins at Bosra include Roman and Nabatean monuments, Muslim mosques, and Christian churches. With all of these historical treasures, it is not a surprise that Bosra has also been declared a UNESCO World Heritage Site.

Citadel of Salah Ed-Din

About 16 miles (25 km) away from Latakia is the Citadel of Salah Ed-Din, also known as Saladin's Castle or Saone. Built in a sensational location on a ridge and surrounded by a forest, the citadel stood guard over the valuable trade route between Latakia and Aleppo. With the strategic view used earlier by the Phoenicians and Romans, the Byzantines proceeded to fortify the position by constructing the citadel in the tenth century. The castle was taken by Crusaders in 1119. Saladin succeeded in seizing the citadel in 1188 after a difficult four-month battle and siege. Among the protective features are a ditch 92 feet (28 m) deep that was cut into the rock, and a drawbridge used to cross the deep chasm.

GOLAN HEIGHTS

Located between Syria and Israel is the strategic Golan Heights. This land feature (mentioned frequently in the news) is composed of a plateau and a mountainous region that is now a core issue of the conflict between the two countries. The Golan Heights is not a tourist site, as travelers are not allowed. However, its very strategic location offers important military advantages because of its higher elevation compared to the surrounding terrain.

Most of the Golan Heights has been controlled by Israel since the 1967 Six-Day War. In 1981, Israel passed a law that made the region fall under Israeli laws and administration. The United Nations (UN) and Syria both condemned this action. While the UN considers the Golan Heights to be Israeli-occupied territory, Syria still claims the territory. Syria's opinion on the Golan Heights is that there will not be a peace agreement between the two countries until Israel withdraws from the area.

Syria is an amazing place to visit. With the ancient history and many cultural influences and ancient remnants, visitors and residents alike have much to explore in the country. This chapter has provided an overview of some of the most interesting places in Syria. Still more exist, and archeological excavations will reveal additional important sites in the future. While it is easy to look back on Syria's tremendous past, it is also important to look forward at what lies ahead. This book's final chapter will explore Syria at the crossroads of time, as the country moves further into the twenty-first century.

CHAPTER 9

Syria
Looks Ahead

I t is easy to forget the future when it has not happened yet. Yet exploring and projecting the possibilities of a country is important, especially when that country has been at the crossroads of the world for its entire history. Not only is Syria still at the continental crossroads—a geographic fact—but it is also at a crossroads of time in many ways.

This chapter will discuss Syria's future, including many of the challenges and questions that now confront the country. It is impossible for anyone to predict with certainty what will take place in Syria. However, we can examine what may lie ahead by scrutinizing the past and present to form opinions about the possible, probable, and preferred futures for the country. The idea of *possible* futures examines the range of likely futures that exist. The *probable* future is the one most likely to exist if the past and present practices are continued in the future. The *preferred* future is the desired path that would be chosen to achieve the ideal or best future. Most countries desire the preferred future and pursue policies and actions that they believe will lead them to this favored situation.

To examine Syria's future, this chapter discusses key areas of Syrian society and what the future may hold. As a nation at the crossroads of place and time, the journey is unknown and could be dangerous.

SYRIA'S POLITICAL FUTURE

Perhaps the greatest unknown that will affect Syria's future is its political destiny. Syria is a country that has been placed outside the boundaries of acceptable behavior by many Western societies, including the United States, and some other countries in the region. The chief cause of this segregation was Syria's continued meddling in the affairs of Lebanon and the country's assistance to enemies of the United States and its allies in the Iraq War and in Palestine. The perception that Syria is working to build nuclear weapons is also a problem. The continuing unresolved conflict with Israel further isolates Syria from the West. This gulf between Syria and the West has affected the country's government, economy, society, and credibility on the international stage.

In 2009, President Barack Obama began an effort to break these diplomatic walls. In particular, Obama sent Special Envoy George Mitchell to Syria. Mitchell met with Bashar al-Assad and other officials. The U.S. message was very clear as the envoy encouraged Syria to develop normalized relations with Israel. Mitchell told President al-Assad that Syria could play a crucial role in reaching a comprehensive peace agreement in the Middle East. Syria also has a continuing interest in having the Golan Heights returned from Israel, another core issue that the U.S. negotiators will work on with Syria. The two countries also discussed reopening a U.S. embassy and cultural offices in Damascus.

More than 100,000 Israeli protestors gathered in Tel Aviv, Israel, to protest against the withdrawal of Israel from the Golan Heights under a peace deal with Syria. The demonstration resulted from the close of top-level Israeli-Syrian talks in Sheperdstown, West Virginia, on January 10, 2000. Negotiations failed that year, but peace talks resumed in 2008.

This new U.S. policy stands in sharp contrast to that of previous administrations that took a tougher stand against Syria. Earlier U.S. actions included closing the U.S. Embassy in response to Syria's intrusions into Lebanon and Iraq. The United States and other countries also disliked Syria's continued support for the extremist Hizbollah faction in Lebanon and Hamas in Palestine. In 2008, the United States even took military action in Syria when a raid was conducted near the Iraqi border to stop anti-American groups going through Syria to Iraq.

In first decade of the twenty-first century, the United States has conducted a foreign policy much like that of a "good cop, bad cop." Nevertheless, Syria still controls most of its own destiny in its relations with the United States, the West, and other opposing countries in the Middle East. The key issues in Syria's hands that will improve relations with others are:

1. Stop all development of nuclear weapons and start allowing outside inspection of Syrian sites.

2. Stay out of the affairs of Lebanon and decrease support of Hizbollah, a group considered dangerous by the United States and the West.

3. Decrease support for the Palestinian Hamas movement.

4. Stop allowing groups that oppose a stable Iraq to travel across Syrian lands and border crossings into Iraq.

5. Decrease corruption in the country.

6. Improve relations with Israel. This is perhaps the largest roadblock that Syria faces. A permanent peace agreement would improve this situation. However, both parties have legitimate issues and appear to outsiders to be persistently stubborn. This issue may be the most tangled and stubborn concern of them all.

Some other positive steps have also been taking place that indicate that Syria may be responding with positive actions to the new U.S. initiatives started in 2009. Syria has increasingly kept out of Lebanon since being accused of orchestrating the assassination of Lebanon's prime minister Rafik Hariri in 2005. President al-Assad has also entered into indirect talks with Israel. Many now believe that he is interested in cooling off the volatile political tensions in the Middle East.

If the doors are reopened between Syria and the West, and peace can be gained with Israel, Syria has much to gain. In particular, a lifting of international sanctions would benefit Syria greatly. Some of these issues will be discussed later in this chapter.

SYRIA'S ECONOMIC FUTURE

The economic crossroads facing Syria is very clear. There is a great threat to the economic security of the country. Oil has supported the country's economy for the last few decades, but that luxury is disappearing quickly. Predictions indicate that Syria will import more oil than it exports by 2012. This imbalance is being created by twin factors that include declining production and increasing domestic consumption. Since oil, along with agriculture, has been one of Syria's two economic pillars, replacing this huge revenue source will be difficult.

The primary options for filling in the economic holes created by a decline in oil revenue are natural gas and tourism. Syria has substantial natural gas reserves. Thus, it has potential, but there are many competing suppliers of natural gas in the Middle East. By 2009, Syria was already developing natural gas agreements with Canada, Iran, and Turkey that may help the country to develop this resource further. Improved relations with the United States and other Western countries would help even more. Better relations would encourage foreign investment in this sector of the economy and also provide for new markets for natural gas.

Tourism is the second area that could provide relief for Syria's economy. Many potential visitors were discouraged from traveling to Syria because of the attacks on the United

States by extremist Muslim terrorists on September 11, 2001. Even though Syria had nothing to do with the attacks, foreign tourism plummeted afterward. With the amazing history and sites that were discussed in Chapter 8, the potential for growth in the tourism industry is staggering.

Improved relations with the United States and the rest of the West are necessary to increase visitors substantially. Visitors must be assured that they will be safe and that the Syrian government is stable. Better education for Americans and other Westerners will also help, because these potential visitors will come to understand that the vast majority of Muslims are very similar to them and are not extremists. As has been discussed in these pages, Syrians place a priority on hospitality and treat their guests with tremendous respect and courtesy.

OTHER INTERNAL QUESTIONS

The Ba'ath Party is protected under the constitution and retains exceptional power and influence. However, some analysts question whether Bashar al-Assad will continue as Syria's president. His family heritage helped him to secure the presidency at a very young age. Although President al-Assad has attempted many reforms since taking office, they have often been poorly implemented, and corruption has spread like wildfire. As corruption has increased, the watchdog group Transparency International has dropped Syria from its rank on the Corruption Perception Index from 66th in 2003 to 147th (out of 175) in 2008. This is a dreadful and drastic fall indicating a huge increase in corruption. Obviously, foreign companies look at this rapid increase in dishonesty and are much less inclined to start businesses in Syria.

Refugees fleeing the war in Iraq also are an issue for Syria. It is hoped that when peace comes to Iraq, the refugees will return to their homes. Tending to all these people is a difficult challenge for Syria. According to the UN High Commissioner

Syria continues to be a non-democratic country, but some changes are being initiated. Many of its citizens still hope for reform, making it a country with a democratic system and an active and vibrant civil society. These twin sisters, one dressed in traditional clothing and the other in modern dress, face a complex future.

for Refugees, there were more than 1.5 million refugees in Syria in 2007, compared to only 3,681 in 2003.

Rapid population growth is another factor that may hamper Syria's future. The country added nearly 5.5 million people between the years 2000 and 2009. Some of this was due to the refugees, but the country also has a high birth rate, with 25.9 births each year for every 1,000 Syrians. This ranks the country in the top third for births each year. With an annual population growth rate of 2.1 percent, it is estimated that Syria will have nearly 40 million people by 2050. Thus, the rapidly rising population combined with the decline of oil revenue presents Syria with many very serious challenges.

A LAST LOOK

This book has examined Syria from a number of different perspectives. With a long history that has seen the country overcome challenges from many directions, there is still much to hope for. While outsiders frequently have meddled in Syrian affairs, both in the past and present, the destiny of Syria is still in Syrian hands.

Syria remains a country at the crossroads. Unlike the geographic crossroads of the past with outside conquerors, the new crossroads require prudent decisions, bold actions, and visionary leadership. For an old culture existing in a geographic region containing pockets of extreme violence and hatred, new paths may be difficult to chart. Syria, after all, is in a tough neighborhood in the Middle East. The country's survival and prosperity depend on new and more stable economic and political directions.

Perhaps new bridges can mend old divisions and help Syria to cross over to new opportunities and prosperity. Failure will only reopen old wounds and continue regional instability. What will happen? The answer is the same as before: Syria is in Syrian hands. The rest of the world must wait and watch.

Note: All data 2009 unless otherwise indicated

Physical Geography

Location	Middle East, bordering the Mediterranean Sea, between Lebanon and Turkey
Area	Total: 71,498 square miles (185,180 square kilometers), including Israeli-occupied lands. Slightly larger than North Dakota.
Boundaries	Border countries: Iraq, 375 miles (605 km); Israel, 47 miles (76 km); Jordan, 233 miles (375 km); Lebanon, 233 miles (375 km); Turkey, 510 miles (822 km)
Coastline	120 miles (193 km)
Climate	Mostly desert; hot, dry, sunny summers (June to August) and mild, rainy winters (December to February) along coast; cold weather with occasional snow or sleet in Damascus
Terrain	Primarily semiarid and desert plateau; narrow coastal plain; mountains in west
Elevation Extremes	Highest Point: Mount Hermon, 9,232 feet (2,814 meters) Lowest Point: Unnamed location near Lake Tiberias, 656 feet below sea level (–200 m)
Land Use	Arable land: 24.8%; permanent crops: 4.47%; other: 70.73% (2005)
Irrigated Land	8,282 square miles (13,330 sq km) (2003)
Natural Hazards	Dust and sand storms
Natural Resources	Petroleum, phosphates, chrome, manganese, asphalt, iron ore, rock salt, marble, gypsum, hydropower
Environmental Issues	Deforestation; overgrazing; soil erosion; desertification; water pollution from raw sewage and petroleum refining wastes; inadequate potable water Note: There are 42 Israeli settlements and civilian land-use sites in the Israeli-occupied Golan Heights (August 2005 est.)

People

Population	20,178,485
Population Growth Rate	2.1% Note: In addition, about 40,000 people live in the Israeli-occupied Golan Heights: 20,000 Arabs (18,000

Druze and 2,000 Alawites) and about 20,000 Israeli settlers

Fertility Rate	3.12 children born/woman
Birthrate	25.9 births/1,000 population
Death Rate	4.61 deaths/1,000 population
Life Expectancy at Birth	Total population: 71.19 years; male: 69.8 years; female: 72.68 years
Median Age	Total: 21.7 years; male: 21.6 years; female: 21.9 years
Ethnic Groups	Arab: 90.3%; Kurds, Armenians, and other: 9.7%
Religions	Sunni Muslim: 74%; other Muslim (includes Alawite, Druze): 16%; Christian (various denominations): 10%; Jewish: small communities in Damascus, Al Qamishli, and Aleppo
Languages	Arabic (official); Kurdish, Armenian, Aramaic, and Circassian widely understood; French and English somewhat understood
Literacy	(defined as people aged 15 and over who can read and write) Total population: 79.6% (male: 86%; female: 73.6%)

Economy

Currency	Syrian pound
GDP Purchasing Power Parity	(PPP) $98.83 billion (2008)
GDP Per Capita	$5,000 (2008 est.)
Labor Force	5.593 million (2008 est.)
Unemployment Rate	8.6% (2008 est.)
Labor Force by Occupation	Agriculture: 19.2%; industry: 14.5%; services: 66.3% (2006 est.)
Agricultural Products	Wheat, barley, cotton, lentils, chickpeas, olives, sugar beets; beef, mutton, eggs, poultry, milk
Industries	Petroleum, textiles, food processing, beverages, tobacco, phosphate rock mining, cement, oil seeds crushing, car assembly
Exports	$12.78 billion (2008 est.)
Imports	$14.49 billion (2008 est.)
Leading Trade Partners	Export: Iraq 30%, Lebanon 10%, Germany 9.7%, Italy 8%, Egypt 5.5%, Saudi Arabia 5.2%, France 4.9% Imports: Saudi Arabia 11.8%, China 8.8%, Russia 6.5%,

Italy 5.9%, Egypt 5.8%, UAE 5.8%, Ukraine 4.6%, Turkey 4.3%, Iran 4.3% (2008)

Export Commodities	Crude oil, minerals, petroleum products, fruits and vegetables, cotton fiber, textiles, clothing, meat and live animals, wheat
Import Commodities	Machinery and transport equipment, electric power machinery, food and livestock, metal and metal products, chemicals and chemical products, plastics, yarn, paper
Transportation	Roadways: 60,522 miles (97,401 km), 12,110 miles (19,490 km) of which is paved, including 685 miles (1,103 km) of expressway; railways: 1,275 miles (2,052 km); airports: 104 (29 with paved runways); waterways: 559 miles (900 km)
Ports and Harbors	Latakia, Tartus

Government

Country Name	Conventional long form: Syrian Arab Republic; conventional short form: Syria
Capital	Damascus
Type of Government	Republic under an authoritarian military-dominated regime
Chief of State	President Bashar al-Assad
Head of Government	Prime Minister Muhammad Naji al-Utri
Independence	April 17, 1946
Administrative Divisions	14 governorates

Communication

TV Stations	44 (plus 17 repeaters) (1995)
Radio Stations	AM, 14; FM, 2; shortwave, 1 (1998)
Phones	3.6 million main lines in use; 7 million cell phones in use (2008)
Internet Users	3.47 million (2007)

*Source: CIA: *The World Factbook* (2009)

100,000	Humans live in region of Greater Syria.
15,000	Early historical roots of Damascus.
9000	Early Neolithic settlements along the Euphrates River.
6000	Mesopotamian settlement at Tell Brak.
2300	Ebla kingdom falls to the Sumerian kingdom of Akkad.
2000	Amorites dominate the region of Greater Syria.
1850	Ebla kingdom rises again.
1600–1200	Hittites rule Syria.
732	Assyrians conquer Damascus.
612	Babylonia, led by Nebuchadnezzar II, regains Syria.
333–332	Alexander the Great incorporates Syria into his empire.
64	The Romans, under Pompey, conquer the Seleucid kingdom of Syria.

A.D.

33	St. Paul converts to Christianity while on the road to Damascus.
67	St. Paul executed by Roman Emperor Nero.
395	Roman Empire splits into the Eastern and Western Roman Empires.
632	Muhammad dies.
636	Arabs conquer Syria and it becomes a part of the Islamic Empire after the Battle of Yarmuk.
661–750	Umayyad caliphate is centered in Damascus.
680	Caliph Muawiyah I dies.
691	Caliph Abd al-Malik's Dome of the Rock is completed in Jerusalem.
750	The Abbasid caliphate moves the caliph's residence to Baghdad from Damascus.
1097–1144	The first Crusaders arrive in the region of Syria.
1187	Saladin, founder of the Ayyubid caliphate of Egypt, pushes the Crusaders out of Syria and Jerusalem.
1258	Abbasid rule ends when the Mongols, led by Hulagu Khan, invade and sack the city of Baghdad.
1260	Mongols conquer Muslim Syria and the Ayyubid caliphate.
1271	Second Mongol invasion.
1281	Third Mongol invasion.
1516	Syria is incorporated into the Ottoman Empire.

1535	Religious protection is provided to French Christians in Syria by Sultan Sulayman I.
1580	British Christians in Syria receive religious protection.
1860	French troops put down a rebellion in the Syrian province of Lebanon.
1861	Lebanon is taken away from Syria by the French.
1869	The Suez Canal is completed, making land trade routes through Syria less important.
1909	Ottoman Empire sultan Abdul Hamid II is removed from office.
1914–1918	World War I.
1916	The United Kingdom, France, and Russia sign the secret Sykes-Picot Agreement, which establishes French and British "spheres of influence."
1918	Damascus falls to Arab fighters.
1920	Prince Feisal becomes the first king of Greater Syria but falls from power four months later.
1922	The last Ottoman Turk sultan, Mehmed VI, loses the Ottoman Empire.
1938	French and Syrians negotiate an agreement that provides steps toward independence.
1939–1945	World War II.
1940	Syria's colonizer, France, falls to Germany in World War II.
1941	Syria declares independence from Vichy France.
1944	Syria becomes an independent republic.
1945	Syria joins the United Nations.
1946	The last French soldiers leave Syrian soil.
1947	Arab Socialist Ba'ath Party is founded in Damascus.
1948	The State of Israel is created by the United Nations. War immediately breaks out between Egypt, Syria, Jordan, Lebanon, and Israel.
1949	War between Israel and Arab nations ends, but without a peace agreement. More than 400,000 Palestinians are displaced because of the war.
1956	Israel invades Egypt's Sinai Peninsula; war follows.
1958	Elections in Syria and Egypt overwhelmingly approve creation of the United Arab Republic (UAR).
1961	Syrian Army units seize Damascus and proclaim Syria's independence from the UAR.

1967 Six-Day War between Syria, Jordan, Egypt, and Israel, which ends with the three Arab nations suffering a humiliating defeat; Syria loses the Golan Heights in the war.

1970 Minister of Defense Hafez al-Assad leads a bloodless takeover that puts al-Assad and the Ba'ath Party in control.

1973 Assad, in partnership with Egypt and other Arab allies, attacks Israel in the Yom Kippur War; new constitution is implemented.

1979 Egypt becomes first Arab nation to sign a peace agreement with Israel.

1982 Syria puts military troops in Lebanon.

1994 Basil al-Assad, Hafez's heir to the presidency, dies in a car accident.

2000 Hafez al-Assad dies after ruling for 30 years; his son Bashar al-Assad is elected president in an uncontested election.

2004 The United States places economic sanctions against Syria because of its opposition in the Iraq War.

2005 Remains of giant camel and humans found at El Kown, a site north of Damascus; U.S. withdraws its ambassador from Syria to protest the assassination of Lebanon's prime minister Hariri.

2007 The world's oldest wall painting found on the Euphrates at Djade-al-Mughara; Bashar al-Assad reelected president; Israel bombs a nuclear reactor site in Syria.

2008 Secret talks begin between Israel and Syria; U.S. attacks sites inside Syria.

2009 U.S. president Obama pledges to return an ambassador to Damascus and begins easing economic sanctions on Syria.

2011 People's Council elections.

Ball, Warwick. *Syria: A Historical and Architectural Guide.* New York: Interlink Books, 2006.

Burns, Ross. *Damascus: A History.* London: Routledge, 2007.

Cheneviere, Alain, Mark Petre, Emily Read, and Martha Read. *Syria: Cradle of Civilizations.* London: Stacey International Publications, 2002.

Choueiri, Youssef M. (ed.) *State and Society in Syria and Lebanon.* Exeter, U.K.: University of Exeter Press, 1993.

Degeorge, Gerard. *Damascus.* Paris: Flammarion, 2005.

Gelvin, James L. *Divided Loyalties: Nationalism and Mass Politics in Syria at the Close of Empire.* Berkeley and Los Angeles: University of California Press, 1998.

Hinnebusch, Raymond A. *Authoritarian Power and State Formation in Ba'thist Syria: Army, Party, and Peasant.* Boulder, Colo.: Westview Press, 1990.

Hinnebusch, Raymond. *Syria: Revolution from Above.* London: Routledge, 2002.

Keenan, Brigid. *Damascus: Hidden Treasures of the Old City.* London: Thames & Hudson, 2001.

Krannich, Ron. *The Treasures and Pleasures of Syria: Best of the Best in Travel and Shopping.* Manassas Park, Va.: Impact Publications, 2009.

Lesch, David W. *The New Lion of Damascus: Bashar al-Asad and Modern Syria.* New Haven, Conn.: Yale University Press, 2005.

Leverett, Flynt. *Inheriting Syria: Bashar's Trial by Fire.* Brookings Institution Press, 2005.

Mardam Bey, Salma. *Syria's Quest for Independence.* Reading, Pa.: Ithaca Press, 1994.

Perthes, Volker. *The Political Economy of Syria Under Asad.* London: I.B. Tauris, 1995.

Rabinovich, Itamar. *The View from Damascus: State, Political Community and Foreign Relations in Twentieth-century Syria.* Portland, Ore.: Mitchell Vallentine & Company, 2008.

Smith, Joan, Tim Pepper, and Andrew Beattie. *The Rough Guide to Syria.* New York: Rough Guides, 2001.

Thomas Cook Publishing. *Travellers Syria: Guides to Destinations Worldwide.* Peterborough, U.K.: Thomas Cook Publishing, 2008.

Further Reading

Behnke, Alison. *Syria in Pictures.* Minneapolis, Minn.: Lerner Publications, 2005.

Carter, Terry, Lara Dunston, and Amelia Thomas. *Syria and Lebanon.* 3rd ed. Oakland, Calif.: Lonely Planet Publications, 2008.

Darke, Diana. *Syria: The Brandt Travel Guide.* Buckinghampshire, U.K.: Brandt Travel Guides, 2006.

Davis, Scott C. *The Road from Damascus: A Journey Through Syria.* Seattle, Wash.: Cune Press, 2001.

Lawson, Fred H. *Demystifying Syria.* San Francisco, Calif.: Saqi Books, 2010.

Quilliam, Neil. *Syria.* Santa Barbara, Calif.: Clio Press, 1999.

Rubin, Barry. *The Truth About Syria.* New York: Palgrave Macmillan, 2008.

Shoup, John A. *Culture and Customs of Syria.* Westport, Conn.: Greenwood, 2008.

South, Coleman. *Culture Shock! Syria: A Survival Guide to Customs and Etiquette.* Tarrytown, N.Y.: Marshall Cavendish Children's Books, 2008.

Web Sites

BBC News
http://news.bbc.co.uk/2/hi/middle_east/country_profiles/801669.stm
The BBC News site provides an overview of contemporary Syria, including information on its economy, media, and political affairs.

Country Reports
http://www.countryreports.org/Syria.aspx
This site provides information on Syria and other countries of the world.

Embassy of Syria in Washington, D.C.
http://www.syrianembassy.us
The official Syrian government site in the United States provides information on Syria's history, geography, government, culture, economy, and embassy activities.

Embassy of the United States in Damascus, Syria
http://damascus.usembassy.gov
This U.S. government site provides current information from the U.S. Embassy in Damascus.

Governments on the WWW: Syria
http://www.gksoft.com/govt/en/sy.html
This site provides an array of links to Syrian governmental and political Web sites. The site also includes links to numerous other sites featuring Syria.

iExplore
http://www.iexplore.com/dmap/Syria/Overview;$sessionid$L5PHPIQAAFX D2P2MN5XCGWQ
Information on Syrian history and culture, with links to travel information, can be found on this site.

Lonely Planet: Syria Travel Information
http://www.lonelyplanet.com/syria
This site provides an overview of travel information for Syria, along with sections on the country's history, major cities, weather, and important sites.

Looklex Encyclopaedia
http://looklex.com/e.o/syria.htm
This site provides information on the geography, religion, education, languages, politics, economy, and history of Syria.

Ministry of Hajj
http://www.hajinformation.com/main/g155.htm
The official Saudi Arabia Ministry Web site is an asset for Muslims who are planning their Hajj pilgrimage to Mecca. The site provides detailed information and visuals on the Hajj.

Syrian Ministry of Tourism
http://www.syriatourism.org/index.php?newlang=eng
The official Syrian government site contains information in English, French, Arabic, Chinese, and Italian.

Timeline Syria
http://timelines.ws/countries/SYRIA.HTML
An extensive timeline of events in Syria's history can be found on this site.

U.S. Department of State: Background Notes
http://www.state.gov/r/pa/ei/bgn/3580.htm
This site provides an extensive overview of Syria's history, economy, government, and more.

U.S. Library of Congress
http://lcweb2.loc.gov/frd/cs/sytoc.html
This site provides extensive history, geography, economic, and other perspectives of Syria and other world countries.

Photo Credits

Index

Index

Author **DOUGLAS A. PHILLIPS** is a lifetime educator, writer, consultant, and adventurer who has worked and traveled in more than 100 countries on six continents. From Alaska to Argentina and from Madagascar to Mongolia, Phillips has worked in education as a middle school teacher, administrator, curriculum developer, author, and trainer of educators across the United States and world. He has crisscrossed the world on his many adventures and has traveled around the Middle East to better understand the region and its people.

Phillips has served as the president of the National Council for Geographic Education, and he has received the Outstanding Service Award from the National Council for the Social Studies, along with numerous other awards. Phillips is a writer and also serves as a senior consultant for the Center for Civic Education. He has written or cowritten 20 books and has published numerous articles. In addition, he has trained thousands of people in places ranging from New York City, Sarajevo, Ramallah, and New Delhi to remote African villages. His work and travel have put him amid civil wars and social chaos to work with people who are striving for a better society and to promote democracy in their country. From his adventures and work with people from many cultures, he understands the importance, challenges, joy, and complexity of the world today. Phillips, his wife Marlene and their two sons, Chris and Daniel, live in Arizona, and their daughter, Angela Phillips Burnett, lives in Texas.

Series editor **CHARLES F. GRITZNER** is Distinguished Professor of Geography Emeritus at South Dakota State University. He retired after 50 years of college teaching and now looks forward to what he hopes to be many more years of research and writing. Gritzner has served as both president and executive director of the National Council for Geographic Education and has received the council's highest honor, the George J. Miller Award for Distinguished Service to Geographic Education, as well as other honors from the NCGE, the Association of American Geographers, and other organizations.